The Changing Face of Public History

The Changing Face of

Public History

The Chicago Historical Society

and the Transformation of an

American Museum

CATHERINE M. LEWIS

NORTHERN

ILLINOIS

UNIVERSITY

PRESS

DeKalb

© 2005 by Catherine M. Lewis

Published by the Northern Illinois University Press, DeKalb, Illinois 60115

Manufactured in the United States using acid-free paper

All Rights Reserved

Design by Julia Fauci

Library of Congress Cataloging-in-Publication Data

Lewis, Catherine M.

The changing face of public history : the Chicago Historical Society and the
transformation of an American museum / Catherine M. Lewis.

   p.   cm.

Includes bibliographical references and index.

ISBN 0-87580-602-3 (alk. paper)

1. Chicago Historical Society. 2. Historical museums—Illinois—Chicago.

3. Public history—Illinois—Chicago. I. Title.

F548.15.L49 2005

977.3'11—dc22

2004022647

For the employees, visitors, and supporters

of the Chicago Historical Society,

past, present, and future

For Betty and Richard Lewis,

with my enduring love and respect.

Contents

Acknowledgments

To begin, I would like to thank the staff at the Chicago Historical Society (CHS) for making this book possible. During my nine years of work, they located and shared documents, talked candidly about their work, granted me access to planning meetings, helped me navigate the city, advised me about possible informants, answered countless questions, made phone calls on my behalf, gave me office space and voice mail, and continually expressed enthusiasm for this project. For this, I am forever grateful.

Russell Lewis's assistance on this project is particularly noteworthy. I could not have completed this book without his enthusiastic support. He helped locate obscure documents and photographs, read and commented on drafts, and agreed to multiple interviews in which he offered a candid assessment of CHS and the museum field. He is an extraordinarily generous colleague, and I will always be grateful for his guidance.

I am especially appreciative of those individuals who agreed to be interviewed for this project. Among those who spoke with me are Rosemary Adams, Bill Bostic, Kenneth Brink, Louise Brownell, Gayle Edmunds, Linda Evans, Barbara Hawkins, Laura Kamedulski, Tracye Matthews, Janice McNeill, Lynn McRainey, Archie Motley, Robert C. Nauert, Doris North-Schulte, Ralph Pugh, Burt Swartzburgh, and Carol Turchan. Special thanks to CHS volunteer interpreters Barbara Parsons and Nancy Wilson for participating. Douglas Greenberg, Russell Lewis, Lonnie Bunch, Olivia Mahoney, and Susan Samek patiently agreed to multiple interviews, often at the risk of missing a deadline or an important meeting. I want them to know their generosity did not go unnoticed.

A special thanks to Bobbie Carter, Susan Davis, Jean Feit, Cathy LeShea, Lorraine Mason, and Diane Ryan for helping me with special inquiries. I also want to make special mention of Janice McNeill, who is the most skilled librarian I have ever had the pleasure to meet. Her knowledge of CHS is immense, and she answered every query I threw her way. She is a credit to her profession and deserves singular recognition. Additionally, Piriya Metcalfe at CHS helped locate many of the photographs in the book and deserves credit for cheerfully working under a tight deadline.

I would also like to express my gratitude to former employees who agreed to be interviewed about their work at CHS. Ellsworth Brown, Amina Dickerson, Terry Fife, Robert Goler, Marc Hilton, Elizabeth Jachimowicz, Mary Janzen, Carole Krucoff, Teresa Krutz, Walter Krutz, Margery Melgaard, Harold Skramstad, Susan Page Tillett, Larry Viskochil, and Joseph Zywicki were all extremely generous with their time and insights. Historical consultants and designers also were important participants in this project: Barbara Charles, Perry Duis, Michael Ebner, Eric Foner, Robert Staples, and Alfred Young provided a useful perspective on recent changes in the institution.

I would like to recognize individuals at other historical societies, museums, companies, universities, professional associations, and granting agencies who agreed to be interviewed. Their intelligent discussions of the state of the museum profession helped me situate CHS's activities in a broader context. Special thanks go to Mary Alexander, Andy Ambrose, Elizabeth Armstrong, Edward Ayres, Rick Beard, Michelle Craig, Barbara Franco, Billie Gaines, Karen Gering, Elaine Heumann Gurian, Cynthia Little, Darlene Roth, Fath Davis Ruffins, Marsha Semmel, Barbara Clark Smith, Brent Tharp, William Yeingst, and Sally Yerkovich.

I owe a particular debt to those who helped shape specific chapters. Linda Kerber encouraged me to write on *We the People,* an exhibition for which she served as a consultant. Her suggestion helped me choose CHS as the topic for this book. I thank Alfred Young for his assistance on chapters 2 and 3. He has an excellent memory about the exhibition and lent me original materials. His most important contribution, though, was as an editor. When asked to review the two chapters, he helped me hone my insights and conclusions. I am especially pleased to have had the opportunity to work with him. Robert Goler helped me rework and improve chapter 4. Jean Baker, Timuel Black, Charles Brantham, Mary Jo Doyle, Patricia Mooney-Melvin, Ramon Price, Tony Streit, and Patricia Wyzbinski all assisted with chapter 5. A number of people read portions of the manuscript, corrected factual errors, and provided suggestions for revision. I credit them for the improvements and take full responsibility for any errors.

I would like to extend a special thanks to the faculty at the University of Iowa who guided the early development of the book—Jane Desmond, Virginia Dominguez, Joni Kinsey, Leslie Schwalm, and Richard Horwitz, whose good humor and insightful critiques helped sharpen my analysis. My colleagues at Kennesaw State University—notably J. D. Fowler, Mary Lou Frank, LeeAnn Lands, Howard Shealy, and John Turner—offered invaluable support as I was polishing the final draft. Melody Herr at Northern Illinois University Press and freelance copyeditor Pippa Letsky deserve recognition for their assistance with and enthusiasm for the project. It would not have come to fruition without them.

My personal debts are as significant as my professional ones. My family—Betty, Richard, and Tony Lewis and Shelley Andrew—offered continued encouragement. Richard and Tony, notable scholars in their own fields of English, education, and art history, offered a careful edit of the entire manuscript. Frank Starr and Matthew Lee let me sleep on their couches for weeks in the dead of winter in Chicago so I could complete the project. Many thanks to Lis Jorgens, colleague and close friend, whose cheerful conversations kept me motivated. Artie Ball, formerly of the Atlanta History Center, helped me with the final product, and I am grateful for his wit and wisdom. Thanks go also to Trigger, Blue, and Smilla for keeping me company during what was at times a very lonely process. Finally, I owe my greatest debts to Jonathan Micah Glick and John Companiotte. Their love and support made it all possible.

The Changing Face of Public History

From Temple to Forum

On May 18, 1989, Senator Alphonse D'Amato (R-New York) on the Senate floor tore up a reproduction of Andres Serrano's photograph *Piss Christ*, calling the image "a deplorable, despicable, display of vulgarity." This performance and others like it began a series of bitter debates over federal funding for the arts and humanities. Three weeks later, the Corcoran Gallery of Art in Washington canceled *Robert Mapplethorpe: The Perfect Moment*, fearing that an exhibition of such sexually explicit photographs would alienate their traditional supporters and compromise the financial stability of the institution. On May 15, 1991, during a routine Senate Appropriations Committee meeting, Senator Ted Stevens (R-Alaska) accused Smithsonian secretary Robert McCormack Adams of "having a political agenda," and he threatened to cut the Smithsonian's budget. Apparently, Stevens had read in the *Washington Post* that former Librarian of Congress Daniel Boorstin had called *The West as America: Reinterpreting Images of the Frontier*, an exhibition on view at the National Museum of American Art, "perverse, historically inaccurate, destructive . . . no credit to the Smithsonian."[1]

Over the next decade, historians, museum professionals, veterans, and public interest groups entered the fray. The most visible controversy involved presentation of the *Enola Gay*, the airplane that dropped the atomic bomb on Hiroshima during World War II. On January 29, 1995, after nearly two years of intensive debate over the exhibition script, Smithsonian secretary I. Michael Heyman announced that the Air and Space Museum would replace *The Last Act: The Atomic Bomb and the End of World War II* with a commemorative exhibition significantly reduced in both content and scope on the *Enola Gay*. Smaller but no less significant controversies erupted over *Back of the Big House: The Cultural Landscape of the Plantation* at the Library of Congress in 1995,

Gaelic Gotham: A History of the Irish in New York at the Museum of the City of New York in 1996, and *Sensation: Young British Artists from the Saatchi Collection* at the Brooklyn Museum of Art in 1999.

The details of the controversies are less important than the fact that, in each case, both local and national constituencies with no formal association with the host institutions positioned themselves as participants in the discussion. They drew their authority to speak from what scholars, politicians, artists, and journalists have referred to as the culture wars. At the core of these battles, at least for political conservatives, lay a concern that cultural institutions embracing multiculturalism or historical revisionism and allegedly associated with leftist political agendas were mounting a vicious assault on the nation's sacred icons.

According to conservatives, the assumption that American history was really about "how a bunch of repressed white men imposed their will and values on peaceful indigenous people, black slaves from Africa, and women" was both foolish and dangerous. Rush Limbaugh, Patrick Buchanan, Jesse Helms, Newt Gingrich, Lynn Cheney, and other members of the political and religious right accused museum curators, university professors, and artists of spreading anti-American propaganda. In the 1994 elections, conservative candidates won sweeping victories by blaming the current state of affairs on the breakdown of traditional American values. With Republicans dominating the House and the Senate, museums and other cultural institutions found themselves under fire. Declaring that tax dollars should not support historical revisionism and sexually explicit art, Congress restricted the use of federal money for exhibitions and artists by reducing the budgets for the National Endowment for the Arts (NEA) and National Endowment for the Humanities (NEH) and by passing Public Law 101-121, which restricted funding for projects that were deemed obscene by the 101st Congress.[2]

Lynn Cheney's assault on the *National History Standards for United States History* introduced another important arena for debate. From 1992 to 1994, Gary Nash, a professor of history at the University of California at Los Angeles, involved six thousand teachers, administrators, scholars, parents, and business leaders in the drafting of the *Standards*. Funded by the NEH while Cheney was still director, the voluntary guide for teachers received wide support from the Organization of American Historians, the National Education Association, and the American Association of School Librarians. Despite the project's careful preparation and consultation, Cheney accused Nash and his supporters of denigrating "traditional" history. In the press, the *Standards* was equated with the same political correctness that was driving the assault on sacred images in museums and great books in universities. On January 26, 1994, columnist George Will claimed that "the Smithsonian Institution, like the history standards, was besotted with the cranky anti-Americanism of the campuses."[3]

Not all participants in the controversies subscribed to such extreme ideological positions, but many did use the wider public debates to justify their right to speak with authority. Museums have always been politically charged spaces, but their elite or sacred status had partially insulated them from the criticism of average citizens. The culture wars now gave these individuals an opportunity to comment on how museums conducted their business; the public debates changed museum culture and, by extension, the authority held by museums and their curators over the interpretive process.

American museums share several common traits, however much they vary in type, size, topical specialization, mission, and audience. They collect, preserve, display, and interpret objects. Regardless of the source of funding, museums are at some level public institutions. Many are built on public land and are supported by local, state, and federal taxes; most are given tax-exempt status. As public entities they have, as museum critic Theodore Low claimed in 1942, "a distinct moral duty to the community in which they are situated."[4] For the past half century, museum professionals have tried to define the parameters of this duty by asking two questions: What kinds of responsibilities do museums have toward their constituencies? How and in what forms will museums survive in this century? The Chicago Historical Society (CHS) provides a useful case study to examine how these issues evolved and how one history museum addressed such concerns.

In his 1971 article "The Museum: A Temple or the Forum?" Canadian museologist Duncan Cameron argued it is no longer possible to think of a museum as a site of unquestioned authority—as a temple. Instead, the museum should become a forum, a space for confrontation, experimentation, and debate.[5] In the wake of exhibition cancellations, budget cuts, and increased congressional scrutiny, American museums struggled to make this transition.

For decades scholars had argued that traditional concepts of what a museum is and how it should operate should no longer be left to the discretion of an elite few.[6] Museum constituencies, energized by the public debates over civil rights in the 1960s and 1970s and by the culture wars in the 1980s and 1990s, went one step further and claimed that they should take an active role in deciding how museums interpret individual and community experiences. In response, adding public service to the more conventional functions of collecting and preserving artifacts, museums tried to extend their public outreach to audiences who felt excluded.

Introducing multiculturalism leads to the questioning of interpretive authority. In 1969, Smithsonian secretary S. Dillon Ripley claimed that museums, if they are to survive into the next century, must accommodate marginalized populations, must represent these groups in their collections and exhibitions, and must think of themselves as educational institutions with specific responsibilities toward multiple communities. Two decades later, writing in the wake of the controversy over the National Museum of American Art's 1991 exhibition *The West as America,* another secretary rearticulated Ripley's concerns. Robert McCormack Adams explained that the only way to attract a more diverse constituency was to challenge the assumption that museums were unchangeable establishments committed to presenting the nation's most important truths.[7]

The Smithsonian's position was not unique. In *Museums for a New Century,* the American Association of Museums (AAM) made a similar case for inclusion but went one step further, urging museums to risk the appearance of partisanship by sponsoring exhibitions that critically engaged the issues of race, gender, ethnicity, and class, so as to become more accessible and relevant. Although the Smithsonian, the AAM, and museum personnel at different times and places around the country have espoused this position for three decades, the nature of this diversity—who is included and under what circumstances—has not been seriously interrogated.

Terms such as *melting pot, diversity, pluralism,* and *multiculturalism* are used interchangeably in public discourse, but some distinctions are necessary. It is important to consider *diversity* and *pluralism* as different from the *melting pot,* a Progressive-era term that conceptualizes difference along only racial or ethnic lines, which implies that people from diverse backgrounds become full participants in a civic community only after discarding the culture, language, and customs of their home countries. In contrast, *diversity* and *pluralism* allow members of distinct groups to preserve their traditions without sacrificing the conception of national unity.[8] Unlike the term *melting pot,* the terms *diversity* and *pluralism* include racial minorities, women, gays, lesbians, the disabled, along with other historically underrepresented groups. The term *multiculturalism* permits and even encourages the coexistence of different cultures and does not require an expression of unity with the mainstream.[9]

Widespread change in the museum world has been modest. It has been driven in most cases by external forces.[10] The solutions outlined by most museum professionals—to showcase the history or accomplishments of underrepresented groups, increase internships and educational programs for minority students, build museums in multiethnic neighborhoods, target underrepresented populations, engage in more community outreach—have not significantly altered the form and function of museums.

In the 1970s and 1980s, under pressure from groups that had largely been excluded from the mainstream, museums across the country began to reevaluate their mission and message. Dozens began to address complex topics, ranging from imperial expansion to race relations. Whereas museums once were seen as places for reflection and contemplation, they became arenas for discussion and debate. Attempting to expand their museum's reach, professionals tried to transform both visitors and nonvisitors into stakeholders. It was no longer enough to target just the narrow segment of the population that typically walked through the door. Scholars, senior citizens, the disabled, the poor, families with small children, students, donors, funders, new immigrants, politicians, members, all joined visitors as constituencies and claimed they should have a right to comment on how museums interpret the past.[11] In the late 1980s and early 1990s they found their voices.

The public equates a museum with its displays. As the primary authors of exhibitions, curators take responsibility for deciding which stories about the past will get to be told. Interpretive authority—defined as the power or right to select, arrange, and analyze material objects for constituencies—rests in their hands. The modern curator's role arose from three separate traditions. History curators were frequently antiquarians associated with libraries or historical societies, interested more often in assembling vast collections than in interpreting the material gathered. Art curators were typically advisors to wealthy patrons, focused on connoisseurship as they assisted in building private collections. Natural history curators studied, classified, and named specimens as they focused on establishing systematic collections.[12]

These roles have changed and the job has grown more complex, but there are still some curators best characterized as antiquarians, who have risen through the ranks, with training in fields that range from library science to education. This is more common in American history museums where there is no standardized curriculum than in cultural history museums in Scandinavia and Western Europe where curators are trained in ethnology. Museum studies programs such as the Hagley program in American history at the University of Delaware, the Winterthur program in early American culture (in affiliation with the University of Delaware and the Winterthur Museum, Garden, and Library), and the Cooperstown graduate program at the State University College at Oneonta, New York, have helped to standardize the profession for historians. They have also encouraged museums to adopt academic standards, with an emphasis on individual achievement.[13]

Museum constituencies tend to view museums as places of authority and to see curators as experts, although they are not the only museum employees involved in the interpretive process. The curator's authority is simply an extension of the museum's authority. The status and power enjoyed by both museums and curators derive from the value of the institution's collections; from the architectural similarity to universities, police stations, churches, and other public buildings invested with authority; and from the presence of security guards.[14]

When museums were criticized for their elitism, beginning in the late 1960s, museum professionals responded by initiating programs they hoped would appeal to and attract constituencies that had been historically marginalized. During this transition, it became clear that curators, because of their limited contact with the public, were not experienced in addressing the needs of these diverse constituencies. Recognizing that a variety of skills and perspectives were needed, exhibition designers, educators, and public relations specialists became involved in the exhibition process. At the same time, exhibitions utilizing social history as an interpretive perspective began to attract larger and more diverse constituencies. Curators often unfamiliar with the new sub-fields of urban, African American, and women's history were also asked to share their authority with academic historians. Scholars became necessary allies.

The culture wars politicized depictions of history and questioned traditional conceptions of identity and authority, and consequently advocacy became a new kind of authority. Curators were pressured to recognize the authority of their constituencies, who used these debates as platforms to comment on and in some cases challenge museum interpretations. Some museums invited community residents to assist with the planning and production of exhibitions and public programs. The era of the curator as the sole voice of authority had ended. The era of collaboration had begun.

While some curators were criticized for resisting change, many welcomed the new challenges. As museum professionals began to investigate the history of marginalized populations, the emphasis shifted from the past to the present, from national to local stories. Collecting for eighteenth- and nineteenth-century cabinets of curiosities gave way to twentieth-century approaches that were more responsive to the changing society. Realizing that the new constituencies have different interests and demands, museum professionals began asking for community input in programs and exhibitions that would give those communities a sense of their ownership of history and, in turn, of the museum. Collaboration repositioned constituencies as experts, and staff members as facilitators. Authority, once squarely located in the curators' hands, became more decentralized.[15] Because curators' responsibilities to collect, display, and interpret represent the core activities of museums, changes in their status and responsibilities deserve careful attention.

Founded in 1856, the CHS has played an important role in bringing about changes. CHS has sponsored multicultural programs and exhibitions, engaged in community outreach, and asked for input from advisory groups. In this book I analyze the various initiatives and seek to answer two deceptively simple questions: Have the current debates over multiculturalism convinced CHS and other American history museums to relinquish exclusive control over the interpretive process? If so, to what extent and in what areas has this position really changed interpretive authority and, by extension, the way power operates within the institution?

Most of the strategies or innovations devised by CHS over the past several decades were designed to meet temporary needs. The passage of the Rehabilitation Act in 1973, for example, made accessibility a major issue for CHS, as for all American museums. Selected members of CHS's education department (the group best poised to implement the new legislation), with aid from a grant from the Community Development Program of the city of Chicago, were invited to make the exhibit *Fort Dearborn and Frontier Chicago* (1980) accessible to the disabled. Unfortunately, once the exhibition opened, the institution's commitment to accessibility waned. The process by which *Fort Dearborn* was renovated did not result in an integration of educators and other constituency advocates into the interpretive process, an evaluation of current installations, or a policy to guide future projects. A program that generates change disrupts categories of knowledge, has an institutionwide impact, and requires time and resources. *Fort Dearborn* involved four staff members, received funding from a single donor, and remained on view for only a short period of time. It did not have a lasting impact on the institution.

This book examines a different, more complex group of initiatives, hires, and exhibitions that resulted in a reevaluation of the status quo. Over the course of three decades several important exhibitions (*We the People: Creating a New Nation, 1765–1820,* and *Neighborhoods: Keepers of Culture*), a new management structure, the shift toward urban history, a building program, a revised mission statement, and the growing visibility of the education department altered how the staff collects and interprets objects and artifacts and, by extension, views history. These developments also determined how and when curators, educators, academic historians, administrators, or members of the community began to share interpretive authority.

Based on the conviction that interpreting museum collections is a form of power, this book examines how and why the process of sharing authority evolved, and more important, the significance of this transformation.[16] A key question guides this investigation: What counts as change? It is important to make a distinction between innovations and change. Innovations are temporary strategies in response to or in anticipation of a particular demand, often intended to avoid conflict. Change is a set of interventions that disrupt categories of knowledge and the current power structure. In more specific terms, I propose that a program, initiative, or exhibition that generates change (1) has an institutionwide impact, (2) requires financial and intellectual support, and (3) challenges the institution's exclusive authority over the interpretive process. These distinctions provide a framework in which to explore how multiculturalism is conceptualized in American museums, how it has evolved, and where the future lies.

Much of the current scholarship on museums surveys individual programs or exhibitions without providing a critical perspective on how such initiatives fit into larger patterns or what they reveal about change over time. In order to avoid a superficial view, this book evaluates nearly 150 years of

CHS's history and situates the changes within broader trends in the museum world. CHS's struggle to reconcile competing mandates to preserve and to interpret a diverse history is instructive, though not unique. While offering an extended analysis of a single institution, this investigation has implications beyond its specific locale and speaks to scholars in other fields. The rise of multiculturalism, the erosion of expert authority, the culture wars, and the unique problems associated with blending popular and academic representations of the past are issues that have broad resonance. CHS, long recognized as one of the country's leading urban history museums, is a valuable and timely case study because it is both at the forefront and representative of these trends.

CHAPTER ONE

Decades of Change

A finished museum is a dead museum,
and a dead museum is a useless museum.
—GEORGE BROWNE GOOD, *THE PRINCIPLES*
OF MUSEUM ADMINISTRATION (1895)

Founded on April 24, 1856, in the law office of Scammon and McCagg, the Chicago Historical Society is the oldest cultural institution in Chicago and one of the oldest in the state of Illinois. A private nonprofit corporation, the society was organized "to encourage historical enquiry and spread historical information, especially within the State of Illinois, and also within the entire territory of the North-West."[1] The twelve founders were prominent Chicago residents who shared a common interest in preserving the patriotic past, a past that offered the new commercial city both culture and refinement. Similar to most nineteenth century historical societies, CHS functioned as a private club and restricted its membership to the city's elite. The founding membership was limited to thirty. Today, CHS is one of the country's leading urban historical societies, dedicated to public service. But accessibility has not always been its goal.

A week after the founding, William Ogden, the first mayor of Chicago, donated the third floor of his building on the corner of Clark and Lake streets, and William Barry was appointed librarian. In its first decade of existence, CHS stored its collections in rented rooms throughout the city, first in the Exchange Building at Clark and Lake streets, then in the Rumsey Building on LaSalle Street (1856–1858), and finally at the Newberry Building at Wells and Kinzie streets (1858–1868).[2] By the time the first building opened on the northwest corner of Dearborn and Ontario streets in 1868, the society had collected over fifteen thousand bound volumes, seventy-two thousand pamphlets, and numerous manuscript collections. The society's growth was temporarily halted by the 1871 Chicago fire, which destroyed the building and its collection, except for a hymnal and the manuscript of George Flower's "History of the English Settlement in Edwards County." The society did not hold regular meetings between 1871 and 1874, but the members continued to collect and store materials at the Inter-Ocean Building at Michigan and Congress streets, until these too were burned in another fire on July 14, 1874.[3] Despite these setbacks, the members managed to open a second, smaller building on Ontario and Dearborn in place of the one that burned. The collections quickly outgrew the temporary structure. With a $48,325.37 bequest from lawyer Henry Dilworth Gilpin and a $25,000 donation from longtime CHS supporter John Crerar, the members opened a third building on December 15, 1896, again on the corner of Dearborn and Ontario streets. By this point other cultural institutions in Chicago, such as the Art Institute, had become more focused on attracting the public, and the private nature of CHS seemed out of step with new trends.[4]

Concerned about the future, the society, counting 313 members, finally opened its doors to the public by 1906. President Edward G. Mason heralded the new emphasis on accessibility, and his democratic rhetoric echoed that of most American museums founded before the Civil War. The belief that American institutions should serve a wide range of the public could not overcome the social constraints that prevented widespread civic participation. Elitism, not egalitarianism, prevailed.[5] The society's audience was similarly limited and would not be diversified until the second half of the twentieth century.

In the decades after its founding, the society's chief task was to collect and preserve the manuscripts, documents, and papers of great men. Because the federal and most state governments were reluctant to become custodians of the national past, the primary responsibility for gathering documents and artifacts of American history fell to private collectors, museums, and libraries. Most of the CHS collections prior to 1920 came from families who had moved to Chicago from the East Coast. The objects donated to CHS during this period either illuminated some aspect of the national past or documented the history of influential families; only a few objects related to the lives of ordinary people.

The society's closest counterparts in Chicago did not always share similar goals. The Newberry Library (1887), like CHS, reflected the different philosophies of the city's cultural elite and became a bastion of traditional values.[6] In contrast to both CHS and the Newberry, the Chicago Public Library (1873) was founded as a circulating library to serve the city's diverse populace. The trustees of each institution, although employing different techniques, shared a hope that their endeavors would attract the attention and praise of more established institutions on the East Coast, promoting Chicago as a city of taste and refinement.

This sentiment, shared by many of Chicago's elite, was in direct response to the city's growth in the nineteenth century. Thirteen years after the city's incorporation in 1837 the population reached thirty thousand, and by 1890 it numbered a million. More than any other factor, the railroads contributed to this rapid expansion. In 1850 Chicago had one line, the Galena and Chicago Union; six years later it boasted nearly three thousand miles of track.[7] A large proportion of the newcomers were foreign born, with Irish and Germans composing the largest ethnic groups. The city's elite sought to use museums and libraries to educate and control what they deemed an un-refined mass. By the turn of the century, many of the cultural institutions had been established: CHS (1856), the Art Institute of Chicago (1869), the University of Chicago (1890), the Chicago Symphony Orchestra (1890), the Field Museum (1893), and the Crerar Library (1894).

Two trends emerged in the early twentieth century that radically altered American history museums. While American collectors had largely focused on Europe, a new passion for Americana paved the way for establishing the field of American decorative arts. The second trend was that, during this pe-riod, private collections were bequeathed to or became major national muse-ums.[8] J. P. Morgan donated his collection of American furniture and decora-tive arts to the Wadsworth Atheneum, Arthur A. Schomburg sold his collection of African American books to the New York Public Library, and Henry Frances du Pont offered his collection of Americana to Winterthur. CHS clearly benefited from this trend.

The society's largest acquisition of early American materials came from the estate of Charles F. Gunther, a local candy manufacturer who was an avid—but indiscriminate—collector. In 1889 Gunther purchased Libby Prison, the Confederate facility in Richmond, and had it reconstructed in Chicago to serve as a museum to house an eclectic collection that included George Washington's inauguration suit, the first U.S. patent, and Lincoln's famous Civil War dispatch urging General Grant: "Let the thing be pressed."[9] One of the more questionable items was a skin that reportedly belonged to the snake that tempted Eve in the Garden of Eden. Lacking the space or staff to properly care for the materials, the trustees began to solicit funds in the early 1930s to construct a fourth building two miles north of the Loop, Chicago's central business district, at the south end of Lincoln Park.

While most historical societies at this time functioned as libraries, CHS was innovative for its decision to divide its resources between the library and the museum. The new 1932 building featured a series of reproductions of historic interiors from sites of national importance. Not surprisingly, the new CHS largely focused on the history of the United States, paying homage to the heroes of American history. The museum made only periodic mention of life in the Midwest with the Chicago dioramas, a gallery on the Chicago fire of 1871, and a period room depicting pioneer life in Illinois.[10] In spite of the limited interpretive focus, the 1932 building helped revitalize CHS by attracting new visitors. The staff utilized two new interpretive techniques: dioramas and period rooms.

Borrowed from natural history museums, dioramas re-created historical events to offer visitors a new perspective. Because the Chicago and Lincoln dioramas were visually appealing and did not rely on lengthy pedantic labels, they were extremely popular with audiences. Similarly, the early period rooms at CHS—the Columbus Room, the Washington Room, the Paul Revere House, and Lincoln Hall—displayed relics of the rich and famous needing little interpretation. Objects were identified but not discussed in relation to each other; instead, they were linked by their association with patriotic events. These exhibitions also became an important way to showcase the generosity of CHS donors.

By the 1940s the society had a national reputation as a museum and library of early American history. The holdings on the Civil War and Lincoln attracted international attention, but it was not until Paul Angle, former librarian of the Illinois State Historical Society, joined the institution as director in 1945 that CHS began to function as a true public institution. Angle's tenure is marked by several significant changes. He encouraged the staff to collect materials related to the history of Chicago, inviting the Chicago Area Camera Clubs Association (CACCA), a group of amateur photographers, to submit their photographs to CHS. Under the rubric "The Chicago Project for Historical Photography," the society had by 1965 collected over fifteen thousand images from this group. Inspired by his success with local collecting, Angle declared that CHS should "acquire no general American historical material except that which is necessary for reference purposes."[11] What had previously been a small eclectic collection of books became an important research center for American and, to a lesser degree, Chicago history. The CHS library was important for another reason as well. While most private libraries were restricted to members or required users to submit letters of introduction, Angle opened the facility to scholars, students, and the public.

Angle published abundantly to increase communication between the society and its constituencies. Throughout his tenure he wrote prolifically and dedicated his efforts to professionalizing the institution's output. In 1945 he started *Chicago History,* a thirty-two-page quarterly pamphlet and eclectic chronicle of the society's activities that served to attract new members and boost the institution's endowment. Until the middle of the twentieth century CHS had been funded by industrialists and merchants Philip Wrigley, Marshall Field, William McCormick Blair, Robert McCormick, Charles B. Pike, and Potter Palmer, and the society's activities naturally reflected the desires and tastes of this group. During these years fund-raising was an informal affair, a lunch with or reception for gentlemen scholars. In the days before development offices, this responsibility fell on Angle's shoulders. He was skillful in courting donors, and CHS enjoyed relative prosperity during his tenure.

In spite of Angle's attempts to build a larger audience, public outreach was often limited to lectures or workshops that attracted students, historians, and genealogists. Publicly funded historical societies, in contrast to CHS, gave education a more visible role. The early years of the State Historical Society of Wisconsin (1854) exemplified this difference. Lyman Copeland Draper, chief librarian for thirty-one years, was reluctant to limit Wisconsin's collections to a small cadre of scholars, and he and his successor, Rueben Gold Thwaites, rejected the academic model for a more progressive one. Wisconsin's attention to public education kept its focus on serving the general populace.[12] Whereas Missouri (1844), Wisconsin (1854), Minnesota (1856), Iowa (1892), and other state-supported historical societies, inspired by the New Deal's emphasis on regional culture, established education departments in the 1930s and experimented with public outreach, CHS was still beholden to the whims of its donors.[13]

At the CHS 1956 annual meeting, Angle announced that he wanted to step down as director and recommended that the board conduct a national search for his replacement. His goal was to shed his administrative duties and function instead as the director of publications. Despite his attempts to change his role, for the next nine years he guided CHS through a difficult transition. In July 1956, Lloyd A. Brown was hired to replace Angle, and Lester B. Bridaham was appointed to the newly created position of museum director. Bridaham stayed for only a year, and Brown remained in his position for eighteen months. When Brown left, Angle was appointed acting director. To lighten Angle's administrative duties, Archie Jones was hired as assistant director in July 1959 and promoted to associate director on July 1, 1962. Convinced that he would never become director, Jones resigned in September 1963. He was replaced by Clement Silvestro, former director of the American Association for State and Local History (AASLH) in November. Even with Silvestro as director, CHS operated under Angle's influence for the next decade.

The 1960s was a period of radical change for America and its museums. Feminists, antiwar protesters, and civil rights activists scrutinized the nation's institutions and intellectual traditions and insisted upon radical revisions. Criticized for their elitism, museums became lightning rods for much of this protest. Thomas Hoving—often called the P. T. Barnum of the twentieth century for his invention of the "blockbuster" exhibition (an exhibition focused on a popular theme, historic figure, or artist such as baseball, Abraham Lincoln, or Henri Matisse)—and the Metropolitan Museum of Art's trustees engaged in an extensive review of that museum's constitution and bylaws. As a direct result of this review, the Met made its board of trustees more representative of the institution's diverse constituencies, hired a community liaison officer, updated the exhibition program, redesigned the building, and recruited minority teenagers for an innovative internship program.[14]

The most visible change came with *Harlem on My Mind,* which opened on January 18, 1969. This was not a traditional art show. Enlarged photographs were accompanied by jazz and blues recordings, speeches, and labels that included newspaper stories related to Harlem. Angered by the anti-Semitic subtext, especially Candice Van Ellison's introduction to the catalogue, which declared that "our contempt for the Jew makes us feel more completely American," the exhibition was picketed by Jewish groups, and Mayor John V. Lindsay threatened to deny the Met's funding until it withdrew the catalogue.[15] In spite of the problems, this exhibition remains an important benchmark. It was the first time that a major art museum considered African American life and culture worthy of critical examination. It also signaled the beginning of the era of the blockbuster exhibition. Whatever the weaknesses, *Harlem on My Mind* sent shock waves through the museum world.

Inspired by the Met's example, museums around the country began reevaluating their institutional policies, interpretive practices, and collecting strategies. Clement Silvestro's tenure as director of CHS spans this tumultuous era from 1964 to 1974. In contrast to Angle, he came to the institution with substantial administrative experience. The society's first hundred years had been characterized by indiscriminate collecting, and Silvestro now sought to systematize the process. By the end of his directorship, CHS had amassed a more focused collection of Chicago decorative arts and photographs documenting the city's changing urban landscape. But Chicago history was not yet the institution's priority, as evidenced by the 1973 purchase of Paul Revere's painting *The Bloody Massacre Perpetrated in King Street, Boston, on March 5, 1770,* and four Amos Doolittle prints from the J. William Middendorf II Collection at Sotheby's. Reflecting on the purchase, Silvestro wrote in the 1973–1974 annual report: "It will be a long time before many of our sister institutions and private collectors in the East will stop gnashing their teeth because these unique prints have become property of a *Midwestern* institution."[16] Although still not fully focused on urban history, active collecting in these years helped build the institution's national reputation as a research center.

The costume collection, popular with visitors and donors, was a key factor in popularizing CHS. Aware of the collection's potential, Silvestro designated gallery space on the first floor. To help fund the interpretive programs, he helped curator of costumes Phillis Healy cultivate an impressive list of donors. Throughout this period the Fashion Group of Chicago, a team of professional women in the fashion industry interested in haute couture, helped raise money for exhibitions and acquisitions. As the collection's profile grew, it became clear that it needed greater institutional support. In 1972 the trustees formed a costume committee to serve as a "separate funding arm and organizational force." Under the leadership of Helen Wrigley, Hachen Stern, *Daily News* fashion writer Peg Zwecker, Abra Prentice Anderson, and Hope McCormick, the committee worked to promote appreciation and a proper environment for costumes, with an emphasis on high-end fashion.[17] The institution now needed someone to achieve these goals. In 1974 Silvestro replaced curator Healy, who had served since 1934, with Elizabeth Jachimowicz, former curator of costumes at the Museum of the City of New York. Trained in history, museology, and art history, Jachimowicz became the institution's first professional curator. She and the costume committee raised money for departmental and institutional activities and organized a series of exhibitions and public programs that drew large crowds and national attention.

Silvestro's willingness to seek outside support for exhibitions and acquisitions indicated that the society's traditional system of patronage was waning. As the Wrigley, McNally, Palmer, and McCormick fortunes passed to the next generation, their heirs' support of CHS became more sporadic. This problem was not unique to CHS, and faced with a dwindling list of donors museums throughout the country began to rely on increased support from public and private sources. Silvestro combined old and new methods of fund-raising. The costume committee and the Guild (a members' organization founded in 1948 to promote the CHS mission) became satellite groups that hosted special projects and contributed to the annual fund. Largely supported by old Chicago money, these two groups solicited traditional patrons. Aware of the imminent sea change, Silvestro also began to apply for federal, state, and local funding. No longer dependent upon an elite group of like-minded businessmen, CHS was now under scrutiny from funders who did not necessarily agree on how the past should be interpreted. Changes in funding precipitated changes in the exhibition program.

Increased exhibition space created by an addition to the 1932 building also helped expand CHS's interpretive focus. In 1970 the trustees broke ground for what would become a $3.7 million addition. The three-story structure, designed by Alfred Shaw and Associates, was completed in 1972, and the space on the top floor of the older building that had previously housed the museum collection was remodeled for the library. Although voted the ugliest building in Chicago and eventually covered up in the 1988 expansion, this addition doubled the space for the fast-growing archival collection.[18]

The promise of a new building inspired Silvestro to upgrade the exhibitions program. Where chief curator Maxson Holloway and assistant curator Joseph Zwyicki had previously worked with an annual budget of about six thousand dollars, Silvestro tripled that amount. The early exhibitions in Silvestro's tenure—*Color, Design, and Heritage: Folk Costumes of Chicago's Diverse People* (1965), *American Folk Art* (1967), and *The Great Chicago Fire* (1971), with their imaginative use of color and technology—reflected these changes. The *Pioneer Life Gallery* (1973) and the *Lincoln Gallery* (1973) would be Silvestro's most lasting contributions. Modeled after Old Sturbridge Village in Massachusetts, the *Pioneer Life Gallery* was divided into several rooms that chronicled the development of frontier crafts and dramatized rural life before the Civil War; members of the Junior League Volunteer Program demonstrated wool carding, spinning, weaving, candle dipping, wool dyeing, and corn shucking. The *Lincoln Gallery* featured letters, personal memorabilia, furniture, paintings, the refurbished Lincoln dioramas, and a life-size replica of Lincoln's log cabin. Audio stations throughout the gallery dramatized Lincoln's life. Longtime CHS staff members recalled that the deathbed story of Lincoln's assassination caused more than a few visitors to leave in tears. Extremely popular with visitors, the *Lincoln Gallery* and the *Pioneer Life Gallery* were designed to appeal to large audiences but had little to do with the history of the city of Chicago or current events.

Although *Color, Design, and Heritage* made cursory mention of the immigrant experience in Chicago, the staff at CHS during Silvestro's tenure still did not consider race relations or urban problems pertinent topics. The museumgoing public was not quite as patient, however. In 1973 a group of Native American activists protested the racist stereotyping of the Fort Dearborn Massacre statue. At the base of the statue they left a small basket of fruit and corn and a note that read: "Let this food symbolize our intentions to record an aspect of Red-White relationships which the Historical Society has failed to record. In the Spirit of Brotherhood, we have spoken!"[19] Although quickly removed by the staff, this basket reflected an important change within the museum world. Energized by the climate of protest generated by the 1960s, the Fort Dearborn activists claimed they should have a role in deciding how museums interpret individual and community experiences.

Although the institution continued to grow, Silvestro's tenure was essentially an extension of Angle's. CHS was still divided between library and museum, staff members rarely collaborated on projects, exhibitions failed to reflect the city's diversity, and outreach programs were limited to school groups. Most important, the institution's purpose was not yet defined. Historian David Kahn makes an important distinction that is useful here when he argues that "the term *city history museum* itself can have two possible meanings: either a history museum located in an urban environment or a museum dedicated to studying and interpreting the city in all its richness and diversity."[20] Under the next director, CHS would finally become the latter.

When Harold Skramstad left the National Museum of American History (NMAH) at the Smithsonian Institution to become the director of CHS in October 1974, he found an institution in the midst of an identity crisis. The efforts of the various departments were not coordinated, and staff members did not agree about the society's mission. While the archives and manu-scripts department diligently worked to assemble urban history archives, the museum continued collecting for American history exhibitions. Public out-reach was solely the responsibility of the education department. Not surpris-ingly, Skramstad was hired to "put Chicago back in the Society."[21] For the first six months, he surveyed the collection, read monthly reports, and inter-viewed the staff to get a sense of how the institution functioned. When the trustees proposed an exhibition on American decorative arts, Skramstad took the opportunity to institute some changes. He convinced the trustees that, instead of trying to compete with institutions that had superior collections, shifting the focus to Chicago would give CHS a much-needed identity. With their support he revised the collecting policy, reorganized the staff, and es-tablished an exhibition program that was more oriented to the public.

In contrast to Angle and Silvestro, Skramstad earmarked a significant por-tion of the budget for local history related to ordinary people. Shifting from national to local stories and from an emphasis on the history of the enfran-chised to a broader emphasis on social history, while in concert with the trends in American historiography, was partially motivated by a financial cri-sis. In the early 1970s museums around the country were faced with an un-stable economy that threatened operating budgets, endowments, and gifts. Canceled programs and enforced staff reductions encouraged many institu-tions to diversify their support base. In many cases they found themselves re-lying for the first time on admission fees and museum memberships.[22]

Attracting diverse constituencies required new interpretive programs and more vigorous outreach into communities that previously had not been rep-resented by museums. When CHS was funded by old Chicago money, it could afford its myopic focus on elite groups and their cultural traditions, to the exclu-sion of other aspects of the city's history. Now, in competition for visitors and public funds, the society was forced to reevaluate its institutional policies and interpretive programs. Although the vastness of the CHS collections made this transition somewhat easier than it would have been otherwise, a new emphasis on everyday life in Chicago required institutional change.

The first step was to assemble a professionally trained staff that could transform the library and museum into a series of discrete but interrelated collections. Most CHS employees, similar to employees at history museums throughout the country in the early 1970s, either had been trained as librari-ans or archivists or had risen to their current positions through an informal apprenticeship system; few were trained historians, even fewer had experi-ence in other museums. Skramstad sought individuals whose academic train-ing prepared them to broaden the mission of the organization, and he worked to assemble such a staff. Persons unlikely to adapt to these changes were encouraged to retire; those whose talents were not being utilized were promoted. Borrowing from an academic model, curators were designated department heads, and their staff members were given the title of associate or assistant based on training and experience.

Professionalism, though, would require more than reorganization. Cooperation and outreach were essential to the success of this model. Influenced by S. Dillon Ripley at the Smithsonian, Skramstad required that department heads read each other's monthly reports; he established a curators committee and used the Helen A. Wrigley Center (1975–1976) to bring the curatorial and archival staffs into physical proximity to each other. This process was formalized in 1979 when Skramstad divided the museum and library into individual collections (architecture, costumes, decorative arts, graphics, manuscripts, painting and sculpture, and printed collections), each with its own curator and identity. He believed that curators' responsibilities should extend beyond their own specific collections. This did not mean they abandoned their roles as experts, but that they became more active in delivering papers at professional conferences, serving on advisory boards, and publishing in their respective fields. By supporting professional development and further schooling to gain the necessary credentials, he demanded that CHS staff members compete with larger, more prestigious museums. In 1977 Skramstad announced that CHS was ready to apply for accreditation from the American Association of Museums. Seemingly minor changes actually reflected a new awareness of professional standards. By drawing on an academic model, Skramstad was able to curb any criticism that the historical society was antiquated and parochial.

In 1974, early in the departmental reorganization, Skramstad invited the staff to participate in an institutionwide self-study, focused mainly on the collections. After two years of planning, in October 1977, the trustees approved a new collections policy: "*Chicago history* is the primary focus of the Society's collections and other programs. The Society collects the widest variety of materials which document the growth and the development of Chicago and the surrounding area as well as Chicago organizations and individuals."[23] Armed with a new sense of purpose, the curators began an aggressive search for Chicago materials.

Exhibitions became the most visible sign of the institution's transformation. While the society had previously hosted six or seven exhibitions a year, Skramstad doubled—and in some years tripled—that number. In preparation of the society's bicentennial exhibition, the staff participated in the American Issues Forum, a nationwide program developed under the auspices of the NEH. The CHS contribution came in a series of month-long exhibitions addressing topics that ranged from work and leisure to the physical growth of Chicago. To locate contemporary materials, the forum inaugurated CHS's first citywide collecting program and helped lay the groundwork for Skramstad's first major exhibition, *Chicago: Creating New Traditions,* which opened on October 15, 1976.

Unlike previous exhibitions on Chicago, *Creating New Traditions* presented the city's history as a complex series of negotiations, making it the society's first major thematic exhibition. It was also the first exhibition to receive funding from the NEH, the first to use professional designers (Staples and Charles), and the first to use a professional historical consultant (Perry Duis at the University of Illinois at Chicago). The staff began work on *Creating New Traditions* with the assumption that the research and materials collected would also help in the reinterpretation of the *Chicago History Galleries* exhibition, which opened in the north wing of the building in 1979, an exhibition that was unique for its focus on urban history. With few models to guide them, Skramstad and the trustees elected to present a survey of the city's history from its founding to the present day.

Chicago History Galleries opened on May 18, 1979, the largest exhibition CHS had ever organized. It covered more than eight thousand square feet and used over one thousand objects from each of the eight CHS collections. Unlike most of the society's previous exhibitions, this one was an interdepartmental affair. Staff members considered their meetings a watershed, for this was the first time that curators and senior staff had recognized different kinds of expertise. A landmark exhibition for CHS, it would eventually become a model for other urban historical societies in Detroit, Atlanta, Brooklyn, Richmond, and St. Louis. Though criticized for its limited focus on ethnicity and neighborhood life, *Chicago History Galleries* helped change the way exhibitions were funded, and it ushered in an active grants program. Gone were the days when a curator would propose a show and wait for the director to raise funds, and the days when Philip Wrigley would underwrite an exhibition. Curators were now responsible for writing grants and managing budgets. The success or failure of an exhibition rested upon their shoulders.

Whereas Silvestro had been interested in improving the society's physical building, Skramstad sought to make it accessible to more diverse constituencies. Exhibitions were larger and more visually attractive, collections became more user-friendly, and publications were more widely distributed. Growth in the education department similarly reflected the institution's changing public face. In 1976–1977 the trustees established an education and public program committee, and in 1978 a former director of public programming for the Chicago Public Library, Judy Weisman, was hired as the chief of education and public programs. While Sarajane Wells devoted much of her time to developing creative programs for children, Weisman established a formal relationship with Chicago's board of education, began hosting open houses for teachers, and opened the Marx Gallery, a discovery room that allowed schoolchildren to handle artifacts. School groups were only part of the society's constituency, and Weisman and her staff expanded the programs to include adults. Realizing the limitations of exhibition-driven programming, she contracted with urban historians to give tours of Chicago neighborhoods; she developed a film series and inaugurated a new program for senior citizens. The calendar of events and group program brochures, an innovation under Weisman's tenure, were visible manifestations of the broadening scope of the society's programs.

Accessibility became a major issue for CHS and museums throughout the nation in the 1970s. In 1973 Congress passed the Rehabilitation Act, which prohibited discrimination on the basis of disability by recipients of federal funds. Several years later, the National Endowment for the Arts (1979) and the NEH (1980) issued regulations to enforce that law for museums and cultural institutions.[24] Because of its constant contact with the public, the CHS education department helped the institution make the necessary adjustments. *Fort Dearborn and Frontier Chicago* (1981) was the first exhibition designed to accommodate disabled visitors. Because the education department had the most experience with visitors' needs, associate educator Carole Krucoff was asked to coordinate the renovation of the exhibition. In contrast to the 1932 version, the new installation interpreted the Fort Dearborn Massacre as "part of a larger struggle that involved the entire nation—the War of 1812."[25] The exhibition signaled both the institution's willingness to share interpretive authority and a new awareness that history was always subject to reinterpretation. Over the next decade educators were occasionally asked to assist with exhibitions, but this level of participation would not become formalized until Amina Dickerson was hired to replace Weisman in 1989.

Unlike his predecessors, Skramstad equipped the staff to function outside the museum. By encouraging the staff to embrace professional standards, he helped transform CHS from a gentlemen's club into an institution that was both accessible to and committed to serving the public. He also strengthened the relationship between the staff and the board of trustees. Previous boards had been involved in the micromanagement of the institution, but Skramstad cultivated a larger, more business-oriented board. Although he built upon the work of several talented directors, Skramstad deserves much of the credit for the kind of institution CHS has become.

Skramstad took a series of steps to reinvent CHS as an urban historical society, and Ellsworth Brown was hired to implement them. If Skramstad's transformation of CHS was based on an academic model, Brown's relied upon a corporate one. Brown was concerned that, in an era of diminishing resources, the society's long-range plan was not substantial enough. Even with a more focused collections policy and an active deaccessioning program to remove duplicate or out-of-scope artifacts, the 1972 addition to the building could not contain the institution's growth. Brown began his tenure on July 1, 1981, with the awareness that CHS needed a new building. Much of his energy in the first half of his tenure was directed at justifying the pending expansion to potential donors. Success would require coordinating every facet of the society's operations. As the lifeblood of the institution, the collections became Brown's primary focus.

In July 1982 Brown assembled an in-house team—Sharon Darling, Linda Evans, Timothy Jacobson, Janice Soczka McNeill, Larry Viskochil, and Mary Janzen—to draft a method for evaluating the state of the collections in anticipation of a capital expansion; to this team he added E. Verner Johnson, a Boston architect who specialized in museums, three trustees, the CHS unit heads, and six outside consultants.[26] The Scope Study, as it came to be called, was divided into four phases. In phase 1, in January 1983, each curator wrote a departmental scope statement, which outlined current activities and evaluated the strengths and weaknesses of his or her particular collecting strategies. These statements indicated that, while Chicago history was the institution's official mandate, in practice collecting was not focused on everyday life.

In preparation for phase 2, the consultants reviewed the individual scope statements, the collections policy, the calendar of events, current issues of *Chicago History*, several annual reports, and a series of questions that all tried to determine if the present collecting scope was appropriate.[27] On July 27-28, 1983, consultants Thomas Schlereth (a historian of material culture at Notre Dame University), Nicholas Westbrook (a curator of history at the Minnesota Historical Society), Stephan Thernstrom (a quantitative and urban historian at Harvard University), Patrick Quinn (an archivist at Northwestern University), Michael Kammen (an American historian at Cornell University), and Gerald J. Munoff (a graphics curator at the Kentucky Department for Libraries and Archives) were brought to CHS for an on-site visit. In August, they submitted evaluations of the society's collections policies and exhibition program and suggested future initiatives.

Many of the society's recent changes can be traced back to the recommendations made by these consultants. Although commenting on their specific areas of expertise, they agreed on two major areas for improvement: (1) CHS staff needed to collect Chicago materials and refuse other materials not specifically tied to exhibitions; (2) exhibitions and public programming should simultaneously reflect the diversity of the city and the dominant trends within the historical profession. Thomas Schlereth suggested that the staff transform CHS into a center for urban history by collecting contemporary materials, utilizing advisory groups to discuss issues and problems, staging an urban life festival to demonstrate the society's commitment to diversity, and collaborating with other institutions. Nicholas Westbrook warned against focusing solely on the Chicago experience. Although it was necessary to limit the collecting scope, he encouraged the staff to broaden the focus of the exhibitions and public programs to consider Chicago's national significance. Audience was another pressing concern. None of the consultants was satisfied that CHS had given enough thought to its constituencies' needs and interests. Westbrook pointed out that "Chicago is now a black city, demographically and politically. Yet that fact of life is reflected neither in the existing collections nor in present collecting strategies." A new focus would help CHS become more relevant to the communities it actually served.[28]

In phase 3 of the Scope Study (September 1983) the core team and the CHS curators committee translated the consultants' reports into specific recommendations. Although the staff agreed that the institution needed to coordinate its efforts through long-range planning, these meetings exposed significant conflicts. The curators most interested in curatorial autonomy defended their current policies and practices. Elizabeth Jachimowicz, Larry Viskochil, and Sharon Darling rejected most of the consultants' recommendations; Robert Brubaker, Archie Motley, Janice McNeill, and Wim de Wit were more enthusiastic about the possibility of change. This ideological split would ultimately complicate the implementation phase.

In spite of their disagreements, the core team and the curators committee agreed that materials should be acquired more selectively, collecting areas covered by peer institutions should not be duplicated, and oversight of the institution's collecting activities should be managed by an advisory board of curators and outside historians. With regard to exhibitions, a three-person subcommittee on exhibition planning should be established to help coordinate the exhibition schedule, implement a ten-year plan, and sponsor off-site and traveling exhibitions to reach a larger audience. Finally, the curators and other evaluators agreed that members of the building campaign should stay in close contact with the curators and exhibitions support staff to ensure that priority was given to conservation, storage, and adequate exhibition space. In phase 4, in July 1984, the core team presented these recommendations to the board of trustees, and CHS adopted a new "Statement of Collecting Scope," which focused on domestic life, work, government, the built environment, and art and literature of the Chicago metropolitan area.[29] The new policy indicated to the staff that Brown's tenure was going to be marked by significant change.

Brown transformed the institution into a small corporation. With the assistance of the trustees and outside consultants, he adopted strict financial-reporting procedures and diversified the institution's support base. Instead of relying on the endowment, he worked to increase philanthropic donations, earned revenue, and the society's share of the Chicago Park District tax levy. CHS received money from a variety of sources, and Brown reorganized the staff to maximize returns in each area. The trustees managed the society's investment portfolio, while fund-raising was largely the responsibility of the staff. In 1981 Brown established the institution's first development and membership office. Once a small part of the director's office, development became one of the institution's largest departments, second only to security and education. Curators and the director had previously identified and prepared grants, but now the development office took over that responsibility. By centralizing the process, a new cast of professional fund-raisers led by David DeVore, and later by Marc Hilton, helped CHS successfully compete for federal, state, local, corporate, and foundation grants. They raised the annual fund from $200,000 to over $1 million.[30] Between 1984 and 1992 the society received $1,744,512 from the NEH to support planning and implementation for five exhibitions. The NEH requires that recipients match their awards, so fund-raising during Brown's tenure became focused on identifying new sources of support. Local corporations and foundations, once untapped resources, became institutional partners. Donors were particularly attracted to the society's willingness to engage in innovative programming and long-range planning. Discouraged by episodic involvement with funders, the development staff also sought to develop long-term relationships with the Joyce Foundation, the Lila Wallace–Reader's Digest Fund, and the Daniel F. and Ada L. Rice Foundation.

As larger exhibitions became the norm, Brown realized that CHS needed to take additional steps to increase revenue from attendance in order to support operating expenses. In 1986 he hired Pat Manthei Kremer to serve as the institution's first public relations manager. Exhibitions previously had been advertised in institutional publications, but now Manthei developed elaborate publicity campaigns. *We the People: Creating a New Nation, 1765–1820* (1987–2004) was her first major project. For the opening on September 12, 1987, she organized a large outdoor celebration that was widely advertised in the press and attracted hundreds of visitors. For the reopening of the building in October 1988, she worked with the Leo Burnett Company to design an innovative set of advertisements. Her work on *A House Divided: America in the Age of Lincoln* and the biennial exhibitions helped break institutional attendance records. For special projects, Brown relied on the society's volunteer leadership. The Guild, the costume committee, and the Architectural Alliance (founded in 1986 to support the Charles F. Murphy Architectural Study Center) raised money for individual departments. The Associates, a group of young professionals founded in 1990, contributed over two million dollars to the society's general operating budget between 1982 and 1987.

In addition to raising money, Brown began to look for administrative ways to streamline the management of the institution. Areas that had traditionally been left to curators—what to collect, exhibit, and emphasize—became administrative decisions. The threat of decreased funding and the capital campaign helped rationalize a new management style, which permeated every facet of the society's operations. Instead of taking Skramstad's hands-on approach, Brown established an elaborate committee system.

While the department heads committee, the curators committee, the collections committee, and the staff exhibition committee had been functioning informally for several years, Brown's establishment of a management committee was new. Composed of ten senior staff members, this new managerial class helped coordinate the society's disparate activities and in turn validated a new kind of institutional authority. What is striking about this group is the exclusion of curators. While the curators committee continued to function, it was no longer the forum in which interpretive decisions were made. In conjunction with the new committee structure, Brown also changed his title from director to president and director and gave his top managers the title vice president, further conforming to a corporate model. Brown's position as president of the board provided him with the opportunity to forge a stronger link between the staff and trustees. Under the auspices of the modernization program, Brown oversaw a $15.8 million renovation of the building, reorganized the staff, began an ambitious exhibition program, and rewrote the institution's mission statement. In doing so, he raised fundamental questions as to who had the authority to interpret the city's past.

The society began a major renovation in 1986, and for the first time in CHS history, museum consultants and space engineers were used to create a building that could accommodate the institution's projected growth. The expansion enveloped the 1972 limestone building, adding additional gallery, storage, laboratory, and work space. A loading dock and a freight elevator were built, and a new brick facade was added to the Clark Street entrance. A semicircular storage vault was built underground to house the society's manuscripts and architectural records. On the east side of the building, a plaza was built to highlight the Augustus Saint-Gaudens statue of Lincoln. The final phase of the project involved the building's interior. Curatorial, administrative, and public research facilities were centralized on the third floor with the goal of enhancing interaction and discussion among the staff members.[31] The construction severely limited the society's interpretive programs between 1986 and 1988; only one major exhibition opened during this period—*We the People*. The exhibition team, composed almost entirely of outside consultants, was able to work around the construction (like the building program, this team served as an important catalyst for change; see chapters 2 and 3).

In spite of the limited access to the collections, the staff managed to create an impressive new exhibition program for the building's opening. On October 19, 1988, visitors were introduced to a new society. Of the exhibitions that opened with the building, all but two—*Hands on History* (October 19, 1988–2004) and *From the Costume Collection: Recent Acquisitions* (October 19, 1988–February 5, 1989)—were Chicago-specific. *Hands on History* and *The Chicago Street, 1860–2000* (October 19, 1988–October 1991) were designed to attract children, a constituency CHS had previously neglected. *"Say It Ain't*

So, Joe": The 1919 Black Sox Scandal (October 19, 1988–June 11, 1989) introduced controversy and scandal as appropriate topics of study. *Frank Lloyd Wright and the Johnson Wax Building: Creating a Corporate Cathedral* (October 19, 1988–January 15, 1989) and *The Chicago Street, 1860–2000* examined the city's changing relationship to the built environment.

From a curatorial perspective, *O'Hare—Airport on the Prairie: Photographs by Roger Burley* (October 19, 1988–February 5, 1989) was the most innovative of the exhibitions. For over a decade, Larry Viskochil had been trying to rectify what he saw as the major weakness of the prints and photographs department—passive collecting. In the late 1970s, and for the first time in nearly thirty years, this department began sponsoring exhibitions, in some cases two or three a year. The staff began commissioning studies from local photographers in the 1980s. Viskochil and a prominent photographer would identify a Chicago-specific topic (movie picture palaces, the Dan Ryan Expressway, industrial landscapes), and for a period of two years the photographer would work in the field, periodically meeting with Viskochil and his staff to plan the exhibition. At the exhibition's close, between one hundred and two hundred images were deposited in the archives of the prints and photographs department. *O'Hare* was the fifth in this series of innovative partnerships.

Exhibitions were only one component of the modernization program. Brown took advantage of the building construction to reorganize the staff. In 1982 he created an in-house design department, appointing Karen Kohn as director. Determined to follow the trend set by the National Association for Museum Exhibitions (NAME), Brown minimized the use of outside consultants by staffing the internal department with individuals who had formal training.[32] Where exhibitions had once been designed by a curator and installed by a preparator, designers were now given some authority over the interpretive process. Conservation was also given an institutional imprimatur under Brown. To demonstrate the depth of the institution's commitment to preserving the collection, Brown hired Carol Turchan as a full-time paper conservator in 1985 and commissioned the Institute of Museum Services to conduct conservation surveys for each collection. The management of the collections was also professionalized. When Teresa Krutz retired in 1986, Brown hired Louise Brownell as the institution's first academically trained registrar and brought computers in to process the collections.

While Brown used changes in design, conservation, and collections management as signs of professionalism to encourage potential donors, within the institution he phased out employees who lacked the necessary credentials. He continued Skramstad's strategy of recruiting curators who had been trained by nationally recognized universities and museum programs.

These were exciting but tumultuous years for CHS staff members. When *We the People,* one of the society's most innovative exhibitions, opened in 1987, employee turnover had reached an all-time high. Continued construction limited access to the building and a large percentage of the collections, which frustrated some staff members.

In addition, two hires helped change the interpretive focus of the society. Susan Tillett joined CHS in the newly created position of director of curatorial affairs in 1987; brought in to coordinate the efforts of the interpretive staff, she radically altered how exhibitions were selected, planned, and organized. Convinced that thematic, interdepartmental exhibitions were the future, Tillett made educators, designers, collections managers, historians, and project directors equal members of exhibition teams. Curators, who once presided with authority over the acquisition and use of the collections, were asked to recognize and share authority with other professionals. In another major change, Amina Dickerson was hired as the director of education and public programs in 1989; the first African American staff member in a managerial position, she became a catalyst. Public programs began to reflect her philosophy that "people come to places where they see themselves."[33] Dickerson's most lasting legacy involved the planning of exhibitions. She did not accept that education was the business of any single department and worked to make educators active participants in exhibition planning. Where educators at CHS had previously inherited exhibitions, they were now given authority to help conceptualize them.

To publicize and formalize these changes, Brown and the trustees elected to revise the mission statement. Similar to the 1977 collections policy and the 1984 "Statement of Collecting Scope," the new mission formalized a decade of change, setting forth the society's responsibility to interpret and present history to its multicultural constituency and demonstrating that its perspective on history had changed. No longer content to exhibit the distant past, CHS was willing to explore contemporary and sometimes controversial issues. The new mission also reflected a change in the institution's primary constituency. Instead of catering to scholars and donors, the 1989 mission made CHS accountable to the larger community.

The modernization program, as it came to be called, generated some exciting changes. By revising the collections policy and the society's mission, Ellsworth Brown and CHS managed to engage in what CHS founder William Barry called "the broad and teeming harvest of the present." Committee and exhibition assignments were, for the first time, organized as cross-departmental collaborations.[34] Decision making became more democratic and directed toward constituencies' needs. Even the composition of the board of trustees began to reflect the diversity of the city, which, according to the 1990 census, was largely populated by African Americans, Latinos, and Asian

Americans. Although the board was still dominated by white men, the presence of members such as Sharon Gist Gilliam, Margarita Perez, Michelle Collins, and Wayne McCoy altered the balance of power. Unlike his predecessors, Brown demanded that all CHS activities be mission driven. Exhibitions, staff relations, public programs, research facilities, and constituencies' needs were scrutinized and modified during his tenure. For the first time, CHS used diversity, accessibility, and service to describe its primary philosophy. Most important, Brown questioned the society's relationship to the city's past and in doing so relinquished some of the institution's authority over the interpretive process. By taking a leadership position in engaging communities in their own history, Brown helped CHS set the agenda for other mainstream history museums.

In spite of the promises of the modernization program, CHS staff found it difficult to sustain long-term change. Energy and enthusiasm for the team-centered approach dissipated after the biennial shows. The funding climate, which had become more tenuous and competitive, made blockbuster shows less feasible. When CHS was unable to raise enough money for *Grand Illusions: Chicago's World Fair of 1893* (May 1, 1993–July 17, 1994), Brown reduced the exhibition by nearly 40 percent. Aware that the end of an era was near, Tillett resigned to become a museum consultant in 1992. In the next year, key staff members left the institution; Ellsworth Brown became the new director of the Carnegie Museums of Pittsburgh, and CHS staff prepared for a period of retrenchment.

Between March and October 1993, the management committee and the chairman of the board of trustees, Richard H. Needham, oversaw the institution's daily operations. After an intensive national search, the board selected Douglas Greenberg to replace Brown. Formerly vice president of the American Council of Learned Societies in New York, he was the first director since 1932 with no previous museum experience. As with many museum directors hired in the 1990s, he was a professional manager. His training in early American history at Cornell and teaching experience at Princeton were less valuable to the trustees than his experience with budgets and fund-raising. Greenberg was also the first Jewish director of a society that had always been dominated by white, Protestant, North Shore residents.

Greenberg divided his energies between implementing initiatives begun by Brown and trying to set a bold new agenda focused on three areas: collaboration, technology, and outreach. In each area he was interested particularly in decentralizing interpretive authority, with the goal of attracting new audiences. Like his predecessors he began by reorganizing CHS itself. It might seem unusual that the trustees and staff would agree to another expensive and time-consuming review when the Scope Study and the 1989 mission revision were still viable blueprints for change, but a careful look at both these studies reveals that very little thought had been given to how work should be conducted and how the staff should be organized. In contrast, the 1995 Strategic Plan focused on personnel issues. As with the previous evaluations, the Strategic Plan relied on staff input and focused all the recommendations on promoting the institution as unique and accessible. More than any other document, the plan revealed the society's reliance on the corporate model. Constituencies were called customers, and the market was the driving force behind the institution's service. The Strategic Plan resulted in an extensive computerization plan, a review of the society's employment practices, and a staff reorganization.

The growing use of technology under Greenberg's tenure also helped broaden CHS's reach, making the institution accessible to individuals interested in Chicago history who were unable to travel to the corner of North and Clark streets. In 1995 CHS premiered its Web site (www.chicagohs.org), and on October 9, 1996, opened *The Great Chicago Fire and the Web of Memory,* an online exhibition commemorating the 125th anniversary of the fire. A collaboration between CHS and Carl Smith at Northwestern University, the exhibition, using personal memoirs, documents, and photographs, focused on how the fire has been remembered and how myths about the event have been constructed. In its first week the exhibition attracted 635,000 users, in part because of coverage by *Newsweek, U.S. News and World Report,* and CNN. By the time Greenberg left CHS, the Web site was receiving about 150,000 discrete visitors each month. In addition to online exhibitions, CHS began digitizing over a million and a half photographs, prepared curriculum materials for electronic distribution, and installed an online public access catalog intended to make the collections accessible from any Internet-connected computer in the world.[35] While this new technology attracted more users and served as Greenberg's most enduring legacy, it did not radically alter the power relationship between CHS and its constituencies.

On March 22, 1996, Greenberg unveiled a reorganization plan that established new work priorities in line with the Strategic Plan. A deputy director for interpretation and education was added to the new management structure. The staff was organized by activity rather than by specific collections or departments, which challenged traditional notions of expertise. The departmental structure established in the late 1970s by Harold Skramstad had separated curators, designers, and educators. The new model was more flexible, recognizing that institutional and organizational success depended on a more heterogeneous blend of specialists with different but complementary skills. Project teams—instead of autonomous departments—were at the core of the new organization. Instead of being distributed throughout the institutional structure and reporting to different supervisors, curators, designers, and educators were assigned to history programs or exhibitions, both of which were consolidated under one director. For the first time, educators and designers were fully integrated into the interpretive process. This new structure reflected another philosophical change; the staff was organized to accommodate the audience, not the collection. This is not to say that collections became unimportant; rather, they no longer took precedence over the needs of the society's constituencies. The reorganization, completed in July 1997, finally reconciled internal contradictions and reflected the mission statement's dual emphasis on research and public service, helping to reduce duplicated efforts and to prevent departments from competing for funds and recognition.

Curators, the group most closely associated with interpretive authority, experienced the most change under this reorganization. Trained in history, decorative arts, architectural history, or art history, curators headed departments tied to individual collections. Educators, conservators, and designers were assigned to supportive, often subordinate, roles on exhibition teams. Teamwork and long-range planning were the exception rather than the rule. As museum administrators and trustees turned to corporate models in order to stave off the financial crises of the 1980s, they also streamlined the interpretive process. Exhibitions, once directed by curators, became project based. Curators joined public relations experts, exhibit developers, educators, development officers, administrators, designers, and conservators as subject specialists and team members instead of experts. The society's decision to discard the term *curator* in favor of *public historian* in the reorganization reflected this trend. In November 1996 the job of curator was divided among public historians, exhibition specialists, designers, educators, and collections managers. While public historians played a role in interpretive programs, they no longer oversaw the acquisition, preservation, conservation, and interpretation of individual collections. Greenberg's model proved difficult for the staff to implement, however, because it divorced the historians from the collections.

The Strategic Plan also focused attention on the society's employment practices. In the summer of 1994 CHS formed an affirmative action task force to review the society's personnel practices. Although the society had an Affirmative Action Program (AAP) that guided the hiring of women, minorities, and the disabled, in practice it failed to achieve the inclusiveness deemed necessary by the mission. The task force argued that "the AAP falls short as an effective policy and tool in a number of broad areas: regulation and implementation, communication and training, recruiting, mentoring, and setting goals." In more concrete terms, the task force identified problem areas: education was largely staffed by women; most of the security staff were men; and, with a few notable exceptions, people of color were not in positions of power. As a remedy, the task force appointed a senior affirmative action officer, formed a diversity committee to advise on the planning and implementation of the AAP, initiated a mentoring program to assist in the advancement of targeted employees, and extended the AAP guidelines to all "who have a formal or business relationship with the CHS," including volunteers, interns, trustees, support group members, advisors, consultants, and vendors.[36] While Greenberg and the trustees took these recommendations seriously, they also realized that diversity was as much about retention as about hiring. In order to develop strategies to encourage employees to remain at CHS, Greenberg hired diversity consultants Ralph Moore and Jim Lowry to conduct a study and a series of workshops.

Greenberg's desire to decentralize interpretive authority is best reflected in the project called *Neighborhoods: Keepers of Culture.* Inspired by the new mission statement, CHS in 1992 requested funding from the Joyce Foundation for a citywide collecting effort to focus on Chicago's multicultural communities. Each community had to meet several important criteria: its population had to consist of individuals and groups that had been underrepresented by the society's programming, and the community must agree to collaborate with CHS staff in the planning, implementation, and programming phases of the project. Although many neighborhoods were considered, four were eventually chosen: Douglas/Grand Boulevard, Rogers Park/West Ridge, Pilsen/Little Village, and Near West Side/East Garfield Park. To guarantee that the collaborative nature of *Neighborhoods* became part of the institutional culture, CHS continued to seek funding for community-based exhibitions. *Out of the Loop: Neighborhood Voices* opened in February 2001, and in 2002 the staff began using the community history model to renovate the *Chicago History Galleries*. A three-year community-based documentation project, *Teen Chicago*, resulted in an exhibition in 2004. This sharing of authority (see chapter 5) represented a new era that challenged the way CHS interpreted history.[37] *Neighborhoods* is important for a second reason; it satisfied funding agencies who wanted to sponsor safe topics without abandoning a commitment to multiculturalism. In the wake of controversies over a dozen high-profile exhibitions in the 1990s, corporations and foundations were reluctant to attach their names to potentially volatile topics.

Neighborhoods also formalized a new kind of authority outlined by the Strategic Plan. Greenberg explained that "the interpretation of history is too important to be left exclusively to professional historians. CHS provides a physical and intellectual environment where everyone who is interested in history—amateurs as well as professionals, schoolchildren as well as teachers—should have the opportunity to study the evidence of Chicago's past and draw his or her own conclusions."[38] In this context the society's constituencies became valued in the interpretive process as much as or more than scholars. Such a declaration would have been unthinkable when many of the institution's resources were aimed at attracting academic scholars for collaborative projects.

Douglas Greenberg's tenure at CHS ended in 2000 when he became the president and chief executive officer of the Survivors of Shoah Visual History Foundation in Los Angeles. In January 2001 he was replaced by Lonnie Bunch, the associate director for curatorial affairs for the NMAH at the Smithsonian and a scholar of African American history. This would be of value to CHS, Sharon Gist Gilliam, then vice chairman of the CHS board of trustees, explained, because "certain people perceive it to be an institution with very old and Waspy roots."[39] Overcoming this perception has been one of the institution's goals since Harold Skramstad began his tenure in 1974. But change—as this book demonstrates—takes time.

One of the most highly respected and nationally known individuals in the profession, Bunch was trained as both curator and historian, blending the academic and public aspects of museum work that Skramstad, Brown, and Greenberg advocated so strongly during their years at CHS. In his commitment to diversity, technology, and community programming over the past several years he has continued the work begun by his predecessors. His interest in exhibitions helped focus his energies on using them as a primary vehicle to communicate with visitors. He explained his philosophy in *Past Times*, the CHS monthly calendar and newsletter: "In a good exhibition, there's passion. A good exhibition makes you care about the subject, and a special exhibition makes people see themselves. There's nothing more wonderful than making history and making stories of the past accessible."[40] In his first year he outlined plans to collaborate with the most progressive history museums in the nation—the NMAH at the Smithsonian, the Virginia Historical Society, the Minnesota Historical Society, the Missouri Historical Society, the Oakland Museum, the Atlanta History Center, and the New-York Historical Society— to develop and share a series of traveling exhibitions. These partnerships resulted in *Eye of the Storm: The Civil War Drawings of Robert K. Sneden* (2001), *New York September 11 by Magnum Photographs* (2001), and *The American Presidency: A Glorious Burden* (2002), which Bunch co-curated.

Bunch's second priority has been to work with public educators. Arguing that most museums do a poor job of engaging students and teachers, he has encouraged CHS to sponsor more teacher training, more hands-on exhibitions, and more after-school programs, which have helped CHS to "become part of the struggle to educate children in the city of Chicago."[41] Like his predecessors, Bunch is driven by the desire to give visitors the historical tools that will enable them to discover a more meaningful past.

Blending his interests in public service and in staff development, Bunch set out to create an institution that would help its staff develop as scholars of the city's diverse history. Unlike Ellsworth Brown, he does not simply want to establish partnerships with academic historians; he wants to train the staff to become public historians in their own right. In order to do this he dismantled Greenberg's exhibit-developer model in July 2003 and put the staff members trained as curators or historians in charge of developing exhibitions.[42] Avoiding the curator-as-connoisseur model, he has a more entrepreneurial approach, which integrates public historians, collections managers, and exhibition specialists into a single division. Many of the staff members in these divisions have interests in and experience with visitor studies and educational theory, and Bunch's new strategy suggests that the CHS focus on community history will continue to be woven into the institutional fabric.

As this swift history of CHS demonstrates, the museological culture has been radically altered by events of the past half century. Curators, once primary custodians of collections, are now expected to share authority with a larger group of professionals. Funders, once silent about how museums did their work, now require scholarly and community collaborations as conditions of their support. Once passive recipients of expert knowledge, contemporary museum constituencies are now more likely to challenge interpretations with which they disagree. Although not every institution has followed the same path as CHS, all have had to face the reality that museums are no longer sole voices of authority. There is no evidence to suggest that this trend will reverse. Despite the problems posed for museum professionals by internal and external challenges over who has the right to interpret the past, these challenges seem to be encouraging institutions to reinvent themselves.

Consultant reviews, reorganizations, strategic plans, and revised mission statements, however, rarely result in permanent change. Periodizing the history of an institution by its leadership often ignores how change actually occurs. The CHS presidents may set the agenda, but they are not always the most significant players in the drama. Instead, myriad forces both internal and external are responsible for the kind of institution CHS has become. These broad outlines of the society's recent history provide only part of the story. Understanding CHS and the role it has played in shaping and reflecting trends in the museum world requires a different kind of analysis, a more detailed and sustained discussion of how interpretive authority has changed at CHS. The story begins in the 1980s with *We the People: Creating a New Nation, 1765–1820.*

CHAPTER TWO

The First Act

> This exhibition is dedicated to realism, not romance.
> —CHS FACT SHEET, *WE THE PEOPLE* (1987)

On September 12, 1987, the Chicago Historical Society invited the public to the south end of Lincoln Park to attend an outdoor celebration of the opening of what was advertised as the largest permanent American history exhibition in the Midwest.[1] Governor James R. Thompson and Mayor Harold Washington urged citizens to join together to commemorate the bicentennial of the Constitution on the officially designated "We the People Day." Set against the backdrop of a military encampment, the events began with a bayonet competition, intended to bring the role of the Revolutionary War soldier to life. At 11:30 there ensued a mock skirmish between British and American military reenactors. After a short concert of patriotic music by the Bicentennial Band, the Edward R. Murrow Professor at the Columbia University School of Journalism and former president of CBS News, Fred W. Friendly, delivered a keynote lecture entitled "The Constitution: That Delicate Balance."

The afternoon program, less focused on the battlefield, included a concert of early American music by the Chicago Symphony Chorus, an eighteenth-century fashion show, and traditional dances organized by Chicago's American Indian Center. After a second military skirmish, the Northwest Territory Alliance presided over the closing ceremonies. In addition to the scheduled events, participants were treated to a visit from a member of the Chicago mounted police dressed as Paul Revere who handed out copies of the Constitution, music from a fife-and-drum corps, and demonstrations of the domestic arts including bobbin lace making, cross-stitching, weaving, spinning, wool carding, and candle making. There were free flags, balloons, and copies of the Preamble to the Constitution printed on an early nineteenth-century printing press. The day's festivities, underwritten by the Chicago Tribune Company, were broadcast live on WBBM News Radio 78.

Almost as an afterthought, visitors were invited to view *We the People: Creating a New Nation, 1765–1820,* the ostensible cause of the celebration. Built around the Declaration of Independence, the U.S. Constitution, the Bill of Rights, the Northwest Ordinance of 1787, and the Treaty of Greenville, *We the People* chronicled how the nation's founders, indentured servants, European volunteers, women, children, artisans, farmers, African Americans (enslaved and free), and Native Americans shaped and were shaped by the formation of the new nation. The exhibition sought to answer two questions: What part did these diverse groups play in the making of the nation? What did the framers mean by "created equal" and "consent of the governed"?

In addition to its unprecedented focus on the hidden dimensions of race, gender, ethnicity, and class in America's founding documents, *We the People* is worthy of critical examination for several reasons. It was one of a handful of bicentennial exhibitions that had consciously been organized to give the public a new perspective on the founding period. Instead of paying simple homage to the genius of the founders, it celebrated a shared national heritage while accommodating alternative viewpoints, something few exhibitions have been able to do without controversy. While clearly innovative, the exhibition was the most enduring product of the bicentennial celebration and was the only permanent exhibition on the Constitution to open in 1987 and to remain on display through the turn of the century. Finally dismantled in 2004, it drew praise from visitors, museum professionals, and scholars alike. It represented a radical departure from the society's regular exhibitions and programming and was responsible for major changes within an institution that, in the 1980s, was not known for experimentation, confrontation, or debate.

Although part of the nationwide celebration of the Constitution, *We the People* offered a perspective on the founding of this nation that had little in common with most of the other commemorative events. The bicentennial was celebrated between 1986 and 1989, but most of the blockbuster events coincided with the anniversary of the signing of the completed document in Philadelphia on September 17. The Commission on the Bicentennial of the U.S. Constitution, headed by former chief justice Warren Burger, who had recently left the Supreme Court, was created in 1985 to guide the nation's collective remembrance. The content of that remembrance, though, would be heavily influenced by corporate money. To control corporate giving, Burger wrote to the nation's largest companies, urging them to avoid sponsoring celebrations that were not authorized by his commission. While this strategy enhanced the prestige of Burger's official events, it froze out other groups competing for the same sources.[2] Although not able to gain a full monopoly over the commemoration, Burger's strategy influenced both who was allowed to participate and how that participation was defined.

In June 1986 Burger's commission circulated *A Guide to Celebrating the Bicentennial of the U.S. Constitution,* a short booklet describing how states and cities might best participate in the events. The commission cast itself as a mere clearinghouse for information, but it actually imposed strict limitations. Local and state commissions had to be created by formal nomination procedures initiated by legislators, governors, or state supreme courts. Once the organization was established, it had to notify the national commission for official recognition. Although heralding grassroots efforts, the commission depended on a bureaucratic structure to codify its control, even going so far as to suggest who should join local organizations.[3] A local commission was to be representative of the population, yet guided by a prominent citizen. Although not explicitly stated, these suggestions implied that official recognition was contingent upon adherence to them.

The commission also tried to control public programming through its list of ideas; half of the 1986 booklet was devoted to suggestions ranging from ethnic fairs to community workshops.[4] By suggesting numerous options and encouraging groups to be creative, the commission gave the impression that there were no restrictions or limitations. Upon closer examination, though, it was clear that, for a program to be officially recognized, it had to build consensus and serve as an assimilative tool or a reminder of the superiority of the American system. For Burger and for most of the members of the commission, bicentennial programs should generate patriotism and an appreciation for the American way of life.

Like his predecessors who had coordinated the 1887 and 1937 celebrations, Burger had no interest in challenging popular understandings of the Constitution and the founding period. His endorsement of Catherine Drinker Bowen's book *Miracle at Philadelphia: The Story of the Constitutional Convention, May to September 1787* as the best historical monograph on the period made his position clear. Largely drawn from James Madison's notes, Bowen's argument ignores the fierceness of the debates; it glosses over the struggles over slavery and does nothing to advance the public's understanding of implications of the founders' decisions. In spite of attempts by competing groups—such as We the People 200, Philadelphia's official bicentennial planning body, and Project '87, an organization of academic historians and political scientists—Burger's version of the past prevailed.[5]

Although the Constitutional Centennial Commission of 1887 and the U.S. Constitution Sesquicentennial Commission of 1937 had not had the same control over the festivities as was enjoyed by the Burger commission, they similarly discouraged revisionist interpretations of American constitutionalism. In 1887 the Constitution was referred to as "the Arc of the

Covenant" and Independence Hall as "the holiest spot of American earth."
In 1937 the homage was repeated. Governmental agencies and private associations sponsored parades, speeches, and exhibitions that paid little attention to
how the Constitution had changed in the intervening 150 years. Sol Bloom, the
director of the U.S. Constitution Sesquicentennial Commission, succinctly ob-
served at the annual Daughters of the American Revolution convention in 1938:
"Worship is at the core of all things."[6] The few critical voices, notable among
them John Bach McMaster in 1889 and Charles Beard in 1937, were virtually silenced by uncritical reverence. The Burger commission's approach to the bicentennial in 1987 embraced this long tradition of conservatism.

Created by an act of Congress, given the stamp of approval by the White
House, and headed by the nation's former chief justice, the commission became the official voice of the nation's memory. Although the National Endowment for the Humanities announced a special initiative in 1982 "to encourage scholarly interest in the public reflection on the principles and
foundations of constitutional government," by 1983 it had awarded only
twenty-one planning grants for such projects. Limited federal funds gave the
commission an added advantage. By 1986 the federal government had appropriated only $25.2 million dollars for a celebration that was to last for
four years, whereas $200 million had been authorized for the 1976 bicenten-
nial. It became clear that any successful celebration would require corporate
dollars and Burger's commission would serve as the gatekeeper.[7]

It is not surprising that the memory of lengthy heated and divisive debates
over how best to govern the new republic were eclipsed by repeated homage to
the collective genius of the founding fathers. Although events ranged from essay
contests to naturalization ceremonies, museum exhibitions were especially popular. The NEH initiative was partly responsible for the proliferation of bicentennial shows. Several shows tackled controversial issues, stressing conflict: Old
Sturbridge Village's programs on slavery and women's rights (April–October
1987), the New York Public Library's exhibition *Are We to Be a Nation? The Making of the Federal Constitution* (April 18–September 19, 1987), the New-York Historical Society's *Government by Choice: Inventing the United States Constitution*
(September 17, 1987–January 17, 1988), the National Museum of American History's *A More Perfect Union: Japanese Americans and the Constitution* (a permanent
exhibition that opened on October 1, 1987).[8] As with *We the People,* these exhibitions differed from most observances because they recognized that the Revolutionary period was not an era of consensus.

Uncritical celebrations dominated the national scene, however. The Epcot
Center exhibited Constitution-era memorabilia in its American Adventure
Showcase throughout 1987 and 1988. *Miracle at Philadelphia,* a multimedia
look at the Constitutional Convention, was on view at Independence Historical Park from September 1986 to December 1987. *Roads to Liberty,* an exhibi-

tion funded by American Express that included one of the four existing copies of the Magna Carta, traveled to nineteen states before stopping in New York City in September. The Library of Congress hosted *The American Solution* (May 14–September 17, 1987); the Indiana Historical Society displayed its collection of the *Pennsylvania Packet* (April 19, 1987–March 15, 1988); the Ohio Historical Society prepared a traveling exhibition on the Northwest Ordinance (July 13–September 17, 1987). Even when these exhibitions acknowledged dissent, they essentially agreed that the events of this period represented unfettered progress.[9]

The event that set the tone for the commemoration was an eighty-seven-hour vigil at the National Archives.[10] From September 13 to 17, the world was invited to make a pilgrimage to Washington to glance at the handwritten copy of the Constitution that was otherwise stored in a fireproof vault. Surrounded by patriotic music and a military guard of honor, the vigil represented the worst kind of historical representation. Instead of encouraging visitors to contemplate the meaning of the Constitution, it merely intensified the impression that the document itself was sacred. By simplifying the complexities of the debates, this widely publicized event discouraged the public from any critical examination of this problematic document.[11] The *We the People* curators, Alfred Young and Terry Fife, had something else in mind.

Prior to 1987, visitors to the Chicago Historical Society interested in the Revolutionary period had access to a permanent installation of artifacts on the second floor. The horseshoe-shaped American history wing contained eight galleries covering the years from 1492 to 1850. The east and west wings were filled with period rooms—The War of 1812 Room, The Gentleman's Library, The Victorian Parlor—and temporary galleries designed for decorative and folk arts exhibitions. The center gallery, modeled after the Senate Chamber in Congress Hall in Philadelphia, housed an exhibition on the early republic. Although periodically updated to conform to city fire codes and for the 1976 bicentennial, this center gallery had essentially remained unchanged since the opening of the 1932 building. The Senate Chamber, or the Colonial Reception Room as it was sometimes called, contained a collection of artifacts that the Colonial Dames had organized into an exhibition in 1932.

After the president of the board of trustees, Theodore Tieken, authorized the purchase of an original printing of the Declaration of Independence with funds from the Frederick H. Price Trust in 1976, the staff decided to reinstall the exhibition for the bicentennial. *Creating a New Nation, 1763–1803* (originally titled *Leading America into the Twentieth Century: A Bicentennial Exhibition*) opened on April 7, 1976, and had very little in common with the exhibition that would eventually replace it. Focused on two major themes, military history and westward expansion, the exhibition occupied the entire Senate Chamber but contained fewer than forty objects.

Visitors who entered the large open room were not presented with any clear sequence in which to view the exhibition, which was loosely divided into twelve chronological sections, each accompanied by a small group of artifacts that illustrated important moments of the Revolution. Apart from the Declaration of Independence and three portraits of Washington, the most compelling objects were military artifacts: Amos Doolittle engravings of the Battles of Lexington and Concord, powder horns, bullet molds, muskets, military manuals, and maps of the Battles of Bunker Hill and Saratoga. Little attention was paid to how the war affected ordinary people. Farmers, soldiers, women, African Americans, and artisans were at various times referred to in the labels as "Americans," "patriots," and "an aroused citizenry." Only in the eighth section, "American Culture, 1763–1803," did visitors get a sense of the sheer diversity of the nation. A sextant, almanac, silver teapot, and copy of Phillis Wheatley's *Poems on Various Subjects Religious and Moral* (1793) were accompanied by a brief label that read: "Although the Revolution had been fought on the principle that 'all men are created equal,' this principle was not as inclusive as it sounded."[12] This statement, the only one of its kind in the entire exhibition, was sandwiched between the sections on "The Declaration of Independence" and "The Louisiana Purchase" and seemed misplaced.

As one of the few open spaces in the museum uncluttered with artifacts, the Senate Chamber was more likely to be used as a place to entertain children and honored guests than as a gallery. The education department trained docents, taught colonial dances to school groups, and hosted lectures in this space. Ellsworth Brown recalled that trustees and staff frequently used it as a reception room to socialize with prospective donors. After the Scope Study in 1982, CHS staff agreed that the gallery could be used more efficiently. A reinstallation was as much a philosophical decision as a practical one. Ellsworth Brown began his tenure as director in 1981 with the hope that innovative exhibitions and public programs could help make CHS a world-class history museum, one that was both inclusive and academically sound. *We the People* became a chance to test both his staff and the legitimacy of his vision.

We the People covered 2,216 square feet and was a collection of over three hundred portraits, paintings, engravings, manuscripts, costumes, pamphlets, official documents, maps, furniture, prints, and engravings arranged into eight thematic sections. It was the only permanent exhibition in the United States that displayed original printings of the four founding documents—the Declaration of Independence, the Constitution, the Bill of Rights, and the Northwest Ordinance—in context. Project coordinator Mary Janzen pointed out that it "applie[d] the fruits of more than twenty years of research in American social history to make real for the general museum audience the abstract principles and remote events behind the great founding documents of the United States."[13]

This exhibition was unique for other reasons as well. Unlike its closest counterpart, *After the Revolution: Everyday Life in America,* a permanent installation that opened at the NMAH in November 1985, *We the People* combined political and social history. Terry Fife explained: "Al [Young] and I were both interested in making sure that political history was the motif . . . this would be the melody, a recurring theme but it would not be the only music people heard. We hoped that in the greater sense it would be a story of social change over time."[14] To avoid the narrow focus on everyday life for which *After the Revolution* was criticized, Young and Fife consciously asked how the diverse populace affected the political process and how political decisions affected social relations.

The first section, "A Diverse and Aspiring People," introduced viewers to the many populations that composed pre-Revolutionary America. The next three sections—"Road to Revolution," "Declaring Independence," and "Winning the War"—enumerated the causes of the conflict with Britain and described the events that led to the American victory. The final four sections—"Creating the Republic," "The Republic in Action," "The Republic Moves West," and "Creating an American Culture"—explained how members and citizens of the young nation made sense of the new government. Unlike most of the curators of other commemorative exhibitions, Young and Fife believed that the nation's formative period did not begin with the Declaration of Independence and end with the ratification of the Constitution. Instead, they intentionally extended the time frame, to run from 1765 to 1820, in order to allow for a discussion of the settlement and development of the West, the conflict with Native Americans, and the formation of a national culture.

We the People not only occasioned the nation's most comprehensive discussion of the political implications of the founding documents, it also introduced a new era for CHS, an institution largely known for its Lincoln dioramas and fashionable costume collection. Unlike the curators of *Creating a New Nation,* Young and Fife consciously set out to demonstrate that the Revolutionary era was not divinely inspired but rather the result of struggles between rich and poor, landed and landless, enslaved and free. Fife explained: "There is no other era in U.S. history that is as remote and inaccessible to people. It is shrouded in larger-than-life legends, obscured by a cloud of romantic ideas." Young concurred, adding that "the Constitution, and other documents like it, did not simply drop down from heaven, that these were tumultuous, turbulent, chaotic times."[15] In taking this new approach, the curators hoped to give CHS visitors a sense of how a diverse and aspiring people functioned as catalysts for change and were in turn affected by the events of the Revolutionary era.

Demystifying a historical period that is still dominated by sacred symbols and godlike figures proved a daunting task. In spite of the wealth of scholarship on the Revolution and Early National period, several surveys conducted in the 1980s indicated that the public knew very little about this era.[16] In a report prepared for the team planning *After the Revolution* at the Smithsonian, "Visitors' Views of the 18th Century," Mary Ellen Munley concluded that visitors have only general information about the period. The booklet circulated by the Commission on the Bicentennial of the U.S. Constitution in 1986 reached similar conclusions. In a section titled "Why We Celebrate," the commission argued that most Americans were unaware of even the most basic facts. Citing statistics from an unnamed study, the commission claimed that three-fourths of American adults did not know the subject of the First Amendment, one-fourth of the nation's high school seniors thought it was illegal to start a new political party, and one-third of seniors did not know that the Declaration of Independence was signed between 1750 and 1800. A survey conducted by the Hearst Corporation in 1987 produced similar statistics.[17]

This misinformation is not the result of a lack of interest, however. Quite the contrary. The Revolutionary period continues to be the subject of novels, feature films, documentaries, television dramas, and museum exhibitions. So what explains these statistics? Historians are partly to blame because they rarely write for public audiences.[18] Understanding how most museum visitors, at least those educated in the U.S. public school system, learn about this period offers yet another explanation.

Few public high schools require close study of the American Revolution, and only a small percentage of all Americans take a course in American history beyond high school. Students who enroll in civics or American government courses seldom complete the semester with a clear understanding of the events surrounding the creation of the founding documents. This may be because such courses are often taught by teachers who lack proper training. In *Lies My Teacher Told Me,* James Loewen presents some disturbing statistics. One survey revealed that one in twelve history teachers had bachelor's degrees in physical education and that athletic coaches were more likely to be assigned to teach history than any other academic subject.[19] Teachers, though, are not the only culprits; textbook authors and publishers also deserve much of the blame. As early as 1796, Michael Kammen explains, textbooks assured students that the Constitution protected the happiness and prosperity of the nation.[20]

Until recently, American history textbooks avoided controversy and teachers willingly complied. Both Kammen and Frances FitzGerald, in her influential work *America Revised,* agree that the pressures on authors and publishers from special interest groups are immense.[21] Only a few textbooks, of which Howard Zinn's *A People's History of the United States* is a notable example, subscribe to a more rigorous approach. The best ones confront students with problems and questions that require critical thinking, present topics in

depth, and utilize primary sources.[22] But *A People's History* and other revisionist texts, are rarely adopted by school boards, leaving most students to learn
from older, less innovative materials.[23]

With the exception of those who were influenced by Progressive historians like Charles Beard and Carl Becker, textbooks published before the 1980s
presented the Constitution, the Bill of Rights, and the Declaration of Independence as important, but remote, documents. Units on the Revolutionary
period were discussed in abstract and highly theoretical terms.[24] Authors and
publishers who took this approach denied that history was an active debate informed by conflicting interpretations. Emptying history of its drama is one way
to avoid controversy. Under these circumstances it should not seem unusual
that museum constituencies, largely educated by this system, would expect exhibitions and public programs on the Constitution to mimic what they had
learned in school. Although much of the national celebration delivered just this,
the curators of *We the People* decided to take a different approach.

This exhibition clearly differs from the other bicentennial events, but
what is less obvious is what made such a project possible at this specific historic moment. Although relatively new for museums, the exhibition's
homage to historical revisionism and multiculturalism would have come as
no surprise to academic historians in 1987. Historians of the American Revolution have, since the 1960s, broadened the definition of intellectual history
to include the ideas of ordinary people.

American historiography can be divided into three distinct stages, in
which historians of the American Revolution were major contributors. Practitioners in the first stage (1890–1930) were Progressive-era historians who en-
visioned the nation's destiny in terms of a constant struggle between special
interests and the people. Carl Becker's *The History of Political Parties in the
Province of New York, 1760–1776* (1909) and Charles Beard's *Economic Interpretation of the Constitution* (1913) introduced radicalism to the study of the Revolution. The second phase of historians (1940–1960) is often referred to as
the counterprogressive or consensus school; historians of this period claimed
that ethnic and class distinctions were eclipsed by consensus regarding the
nation's primary objectives and values. Edmund S. Morgan, Bernard Bailyn,
and Benjamin Wright, influenced by cold war politics, focused on modera-
tion and tried to prove that class conflict and economic self-interest should
be deemphasized. The search for a single, essential national character dominated the thinking of this second phase.[25]

The events of the late 1960s then radically altered the practice of American history and the understanding of the American Revolution. This third
period, dominated by social historians dedicated to looking at history from
below, reflected major changes in attitudes, methodologies, and uses of evidence. These historians paid attention to new aspects of the experiences of

ordinary people, aspects that could be uncovered with sophisticated statistical methods, oral histories, analysis of artifacts, and surveys of other nontraditional sources. Social history did more than argue that ordinary people had a history; it demonstrated that they should be thought of as actors in, not passive recipients of, change.

Whether by choice or necessity, the study of ordinary people took on a decidedly pluralistic flavor. For scholars of the American Revolution, this meant a reevaluation of Progressive-era historians' attention to conflict and a new emphasis on the experiences of those who left few records. Three collections of essays, edited by Alfred F. Young in the series Explorations in the History of American Radicalism, defined the voice of this third generation. The first in the series, a collection of essays entitled *Dissent: Explorations in the History of American Radicalism* (1968), included a seminal essay by Jesse Lemisch, "The Radicalism of the Inarticulate: Merchant Seamen in the Politics of Revolutionary America," in which Lemisch argued that scholars should examine the Revolution "from the bottom up," rejecting both that the average citizens shared ideas with the elite and that they formed a mindless mob.[26] Lemisch, along with many of the authors in the collection, argued that scholars cannot fully understand the implications of the founding period without looking at the experiences of the diverse populace. The second volume, *The American Revolution: Explorations in the History of American Radicalism* (1976), focused on radical themes (rural and urban rebellions, political economy, evangelical religion, and the experiences of African Americans, women, and Native Americans) prior to the Revolution. Many of the contributors produced volumes that have since become standards in the field.[27] The contributors to the third volume, *Beyond the American Revolution: Explorations in the History of American Radicalism* (1983), examined the perspective of Americans who found that the Revolution did not measure up to their hopes and dreams.[28] Although this attention to diversity was a new—and in some cases unwelcome—phenomenon for museum professionals trained before the advent of the new social and political history, it became a key component of the interpretive programs at CHS in the 1980s.

In 1982 key members of the staff at CHS believed that museumgoers who had come of age in the 1960s and 1970s would agree that the formation of the new nation required more than the talents and sacrifices of white, elite men. But the exhibition did more than demonstrate that women or free African Americans were present. It argued that the history of the nation is inextricably linked to the behavior and treatment of these groups.

Young authored the exhibition script, but this line of argument owed much to the generation of scholars who debunked the notion that all Americans agreed upon the meaning of the Revolution. When asked which scholars influenced the script, Young named many who anticipated or accepted

Lemisch's challenge, including Herbert Aptheker, Benjamin Quarles, Eugene Genovese, Herbert Gutman, Ira Berlin, Linda Kerber, Mary Beth Norton, Roger Butterfield, Sidney Kaplan, Linda DePauw and Conover Hunt, Barbara Graymont, Wilcomb Washburn, Gary Nash, and Helen Tanner.[29] Although focused on specific topics, each of these scholars insisted that attention to the voiceless required historians to rethink the meaning of the American Revolution as a whole. By applying the fruits of this scholarship to an extraordinary collection of two- and three-dimensional artifacts at CHS, Young realized that the We the People team was engaged in a project with few precedents.

Integrating contemporary historical arguments into a museum exhibition, especially one focused on a period that is primarily understood through its mythic symbols, is more difficult than it might seem. While most curators and museum personnel agree that museums have always been highly politicized spaces, constituencies often expect museums to be above such conflict. Museums function as ritual sites where visitors are expected to exercise their civic pride.[30] Museum professionals who try to expose the power of that cultural sign by bringing the forum inside the temple also ask their patrons to take a more critical view of the past, something they are seldom equipped or willing to do. It is in this context that the bicentennial events of 1987 should be situated.

Most of the exhibitions that opened for the bicentennial of the Constitution highlighted what united the nation, rather than what divided it. One notable exception, A More Perfect Union: Japanese Americans and the United States Constitution at the National Museum of American History at the Smithsonian, questioned the constitutionality of internment camps during World War II. But this exhibition opened on October 1, 1987, nearly a month after the actual anniversary date, because the NMAH recognized that commemorative events are seen as times for celebration, not demystification.[31] Most of the participants in the bicentennial hoped to rededicate themselves to the principles of the Constitution by paying homage to a few extraordinary individuals. Few were prepared to participate in discussions about the limits of the founders' vision. Although We the People was in concert with trends in historical scholarship, the curators also recognized that Constitution- and hero-worship were important parts of the nation's understanding of this period. Young explained that the exhibition "offer[ed] an example of one way several American historians attempted to resolve the polarity posed in the call for contributions: between the protagonists of a new history which is multi-cultural and democratic in its inspiration; and emphasizes the history of everyday life and the self-styled traditionalists who demand restoration of the nation to the center of the curriculum, and a history which turns on great events (and great men)."[32] He did not see it as a choice of one approach over another, but instead as a way to combine the two.

The team clearly recognized that the message of *We the People* was inextricably tied to the medium of communication. A museum has a different relationship to its constituencies than a textbook or a monograph does, and different museums offer different kinds of truths. Art museums are first and foremost places of contemplation, more likely than other types of museums to resemble shrines and temples. The experience is intended to be an individual one. Art objects are often assumed to speak for themselves, and art historians are constantly battling over how much information is necessary for the public to relate to a particular piece. Science museums tend to emphasize a more collective experience, one that promises to reveal natural laws to the uninitiated. Whereas art museums tolerate multiple interpretations within certain proscribed limits, science museums are based on specific, seemingly immutable laws. History museums offer a very different experience. Few historical artifacts have been created for display, so they often require longer labels and more context than either science or art objects. Historical exhibitions are more likely to be organized to tell a particular story than exhibitions in other types of museums, and historians, particularly those influenced by recent trends, are less willing to assert they are searching for the truth. Exhibitions, then, are stories about the past that change with each new generation. In spite of this awareness, visitors believe that what is presented in a museum is the literal truth, not a perspective or an argument.[33] Had Young and Fife not considered what the Revolution meant to the museum's various constituencies, CHS might have found itself embroiled in controversy.

The most important lesson to be learned from the recent controversies generated by exhibitions (see the introduction) is that museum professionals and their constituencies often have conflicting ideas about what purpose museums should serve.[34] Most museumgoers are not prepared to embrace historical revisionism; they typically are unaware that historical interpretations change as new theoretical models are advanced or new evidence is uncovered. They remember what they learned in high school and college civics, American government, and history classes. They assume that what they were taught was the truth, not part of a larger debate. So how did CHS manage to present a revisionist interpretation of the Revolutionary period, which demanded that visitors rethink their understanding of this period, without generating controversy? One way to answer this question is to take a careful look at how the exhibition was organized by the CHS staff and consultants and how it was understood by its visitors.

CHAPTER THREE

We the People
as an Agent of Change

We learned to walk the tightrope...

informing people without being condescending.

—TERRY FIFE, JANUARY 12, 1996

The American history collections have always been an important part of the Chicago Historical Society's identity, and for most of the institution's early history, exhibitions focused on the Civil War, Lincoln, the early republic, and frontier life. Local history took a back seat to narratives seeking to explain the national character. Even when the institution formally shifted its collecting focus to Chicago history in 1977, the trustees were reluctant to abandon American national history altogether because they had one of the finest collections of Americana in the nation. But the first printing of the 1795 Treaty of Greenville, an original copy of the Declaration of Independence, and the first public printing of the Constitution did not generate much enthusiasm among the staff. Many of the curators had been hired in the 1970s with the understanding that Chicago history was the institution's new priority; they were reluctant to support continued collecting in Americana because it represented an antiquarianism they were struggling against.

Without the backing of the curatorial staff, Ellsworth Brown realized that exhibiting the early American materials would require external support. When the NEH, early in 1982, invited museums to submit proposals for the bicentennial of the Constitution, Brown realized that CHS was well positioned to compete for federal funds because it was the repository of the region's largest holdings of Early National materials. *We the People: Creating A New Nation, 1765–1820* would become to CHS in the 1980s what the

Chicago History Galleries was to the institution in the 1970s—a visible, public statement of the director's philosophical commitments and the institution's direction.

By the end of October 1982, *We the People* had hired four consultants (Fath Davis Ruffins, John Kaminski, Richard Leffler, and Wilcomb Washburn), a design team (Staples and Charles), and a project coordinator (Mary Janzen), but it still lacked a curator. None of the curatorial staff specialized in the Revolutionary period, so Janzen and Brown agreed to look outside CHS. They selected Alfred Young, a professor of history at Northern Illinois University who was a pioneer in the political and social history of the Revolutionary period and was familiar with the problems of working with primary sources. Terry Fife, a student of Young's who had recently completed her master's degree at Northern Illinois, joined the project team as the exhibition's co-curator in January 1983. Although it was not the first time CHS had used academic consultants, it was the first time that academic historians served as curators of an exhibition.

Preparation of the NEH planning grant for the exhibition began in the fall of 1982. During the early stages, Janzen worked to recruit in-house staff to help locate materials and comment on drafts of the script. While the planning team provided practical advice, they left the creative thinking about content to the outside consultants. The exhibition team originally intended to retain the name of the 1976 installation, *Creating a New Nation, 1763–1818,* but to juxtapose the contributions and aspirations of the founders with those of ordinary people. In April 1983 Janzen submitted a planning grant to the NEH, and in December CHS was awarded fifteen thousand dollars. This money was used to pay Young for his work on the preliminary draft of the script, Staples and Charles for their conceptual design and floor plan, and the consultants for participating in a daylong meeting.

On January 16, 1984, Richard Leffler, John Kaminski, Fath Davis Ruffins, Helen Hornbeck Tanner (who had replaced Wilcomb Washburn), Ellsworth Brown, the exhibition team, and selected members of the in-house planning committee met in the Senate Chamber to view the collections and discuss Young's thirty-seven-page script. All the consultants agreed that the script did not have enough information on Loyalists, yeoman farmers, merchants, women, Native Americans, and the geographical range of the war. Richard Leffler repeatedly questioned the wisdom of relying solely on CHS collections, arguing that history was too important to be beholden to the whims of generations of amateur collectors. Ruffins argued that visual images of marginalized groups, though difficult to locate, were essential. If CHS did not own such materials, they should consider using reproductions. The consultants were also concerned that the exhibition team had not been specific enough about their intended audience. Leffler raised this point again in a letter several days later: "The 'Level' being aimed at may be too broad. Is it possible to 'communicate' to an audience ranging from elementary-school children to 'sophisticated adults'?"[1] Instead of borrowing materials, the exhibition team engaged in a more comprehensive search of the three-dimensional collections within the CHS. Under pressure from the designers to use authentic artifacts, they did not use visual reproductions. The debates over audience were eventually settled, and the team agreed that instead of trying to appeal to every potential visitor, the ideal was a self-guided adult.[2] The next day, after consulting with Barbara Charles about the conceptual design, Janzen, Young, and Fife agreed that filling in the gaps identified by the consultants should be their top priority.

During the winter and spring of 1983–1984, Fife worked to locate artifacts to support Young's script. As an outsider, she had some problems negotiating access to certain collections because costumes, conservation, and graphics imposed restrictions on the use of materials. Mary Janzen explained: "On a daily basis, [Fife underwent] . . . psychological warfare with curators, including some project supporters, over access to materials in their custody."[3] The exhibition progressed, however, and Ellsworth Brown elected to move it from the 1,650-square-foot Senate Chamber to the 2,216-square-foot west wing, previously used for decorative and folk arts shows, which made it possible for CHS to install a companion gallery on the Civil War in the Senate Chamber and east wing. The hope was that both exhibitions, when completed, would provide access to a century's worth of American history.

While working on the implementation grant, Janzen, Young, and Fife became increasingly concerned that an exhibition focused on race, ethnicity, gender, and class was not going to be funded by an organization headed by a vocal conservative. In a 1989 article reflecting on the experience of working on We the People, Janzen explained that NEH chairman William Bennett "made us apprehensive that the panel that judged our proposal might be hostile to this approach, so we soft-pedaled the essential social history component of the implementation proposal we submitted in June 1984— ironically it was rejected." Young agreed that the proposal was "timid" and "did not do the new history sharply enough."[4] Though it was difficult to pinpoint the exact reason why the proposal was denied funding, the team's assumption that the NEH staff and review panel judges would reject a script raising questions about multiculturalism was incorrect.

The fifteen thousand dollars from the NEH barely covered the planning stages, and the failure of the first implementation grant in November 1984 put the project in a very tenuous position. Since this was a soft-money project, an in-house project funded with outside money, the team had little reason to expect institutional support. Without the promise of outside money, We the People needed internal funding to continue, which put Ellsworth

Brown in the awkward position of having to pay for a permanent exhibition in the middle of the fiscal year while involved in a $15.9 million capital expansion program. Late that fall, Brown and the trustees met to determine how important the exhibition was to the institution. Encouraged by the criticism from the NEH reviewers of the first implementation grant and determined to rebuild the American history wing, they reallocated general operating funds regardless of the outcome of the second implementation grant. With a guarantee from Brown and CHS early in 1985, the exhibition team recruited historians Garry Wills and Linda Kerber as additional consultants and reworked the implementation grant for a June 1985 deadline.

The second script was more focused than the first. When the first script was denied funding, Young and Fife began to scour the costumes and decorative arts collections for objects and documents that would convey a sense of everyday life.[5] The team also turned to other institutions for ideas. As early as 1983 Janzen, Young, and Fife had consulted with curators outside CHS; they read exhibition catalogs and brochures and visited other exhibitions and museums to get ideas. The team was particularly influenced by two exhibitions: one, a traveling exhibition on view at CHS from January 17 to February 20, 1977, entitled *Remember the Ladies: Women in America, 1750–1815,* and the other, *After the Revolution,* which opened at the NMAH in November 1985. *Remember the Ladies* was useful because it addressed how disenfranchised groups experienced the Revolution and provided a good model for displaying domestic artifacts without erasing women's intellectual and political lives. Young and Fife visited *After the Revolution* several times to study the installation and to confer with its curators. Although the team did not borrow many concepts from this installation, it remained a useful model.

These two exhibitions gave the team some creative ideas, whereas most exhibitions celebrating the bicentennial of the Constitution showed them what they did not want. Janzen and Young visited *Miracle at Philadelphia* and were disappointed with its lack of critical engagement. Fife traveled to Washington to see *The American Experiment: Creating the Constitution* at the National Archives and was surprised by its inaccessibility. She complained that the curators had placed all the documents under green glass, which made them virtually unreadable. From a design perspective, the National Archives' exclusive use of marble was intimidating.

Armed with a clear sense of purpose, the exhibition team submitted a revised implementation grant to the NEH in June, and six months later the CHS was awarded two hundred thousand dollars, and seventy-five thousand in matching funds. With the NEH stamp of approval, CHS staff began investigating additional funding sources. During 1986 Janzen wrote supplementary grant proposals and helped the development office solicit additional donors. The NEH grant was a public endorsement of the exhibition's quality and had a direct impact on the solicitation of gifts from the private sector. The Chicago Council of Fine Arts awarded CHS sixteen thousand dollars; the Prince Charitable Trust and the Rice Foundation gave two hundred thousand and seventy-five thousand, respectively. An additional gift from the Guild brought the total to nearly six hundred thousand dollars. The remainder was met by the society's operating funds.[6]

In January 1986 Fife, Janzen, and Young began the implementation phase by reviewing the evaluation sheets completed by the NEH panelists, searching for additional artifacts, and revising the script and floor plan. By the end of the year the team had begun the laborious process of organizing each section. The final product does not betray the struggles over interpretive authority that became more acute as the five-person exhibition team swelled to a crew of nearly thirty. In each section the curators, designers, and CHS staff members struggled to balance accuracy with accessibility. Decisions concerning how the exhibition should be mounted revealed that exhibitions are often influenced by competing forces. Space and available funds were the most obvious limitations, but conflicts over inclusion or presentation of specific artifacts were also closely tied to questions of authority. Mary Janzen explained: "What may surprise historians is that most of the struggles for control were not over issues of historical interpretation."[7] After the funding was secured, CHS staff, trustees, or funders did not pressure the curators to modify interpretations. The struggles over interpretive authority had more to do with professional boundaries than with debates over ideas.

Restrictions placed by the graphics department and the conservators on the use of materials allowed CHS staff to exert professional influence over what appeared to be challenges to their authority. Educators and designers constantly questioned the curators' ability to translate complex historical arguments into an exhibition that would appeal to nonacademics. Familiar with the limitations of the exhibition format, CHS educator Carole Krucoff urged the curators to present the material in such a way that it was easy to understand, which meant writing clear, concise labels and supplementing them with audiovisual materials. Staples and Charles proposed design solutions that would bring the two-dimensional materials to life. But accessibility occasionally resulted in simplistic interpretations. The introductory tableau—a composite image of a mother holding a child, two children reading, an artisan hammering gold, an enslaved woman carrying water, and a wealthy patriot—was a good example. Although it was aesthetically pleasing, the image was not historically accurate. The label copy raised questions about the role played by the diverse citizenry in the creation of the new nation, but in the end the visual image was more powerful. Museum exhibitions, like all cultural productions, are embedded in the politics that give rise to professional boundaries. In this case these struggles were particularly acute because, under Ellsworth

Brown, conservation, education, and design were given institutional imprimatur for the first time in the society's history.

The struggles over interpretation in *We the People* reveal that academic historians and museum professionals often have very different ideas about what counts as history. Academic historians have frequently derided history museum professionals for presenting inaccurate, romanticized views of the past; museum professionals have accused their academic counterparts of using such complex theories that their interpretations are not widely understood.[8] This same tension played out in *We the People*. Young and Fife were mainly concerned with the facts; Staples and Charles knew that historical accuracy did not by itself make a good exhibition. A balance between the two perspectives was not easy to achieve. The most appealing sections often presented a visual narrative that worked against the curators' interpretation; dull and pedantic parts of the exhibition often contained the most sophisticated historical insights. The final product reflected more an uneasy truce among members of the exhibition team than a genuine collaboration, and so it is important also to assess how the visitors understood the exhibition.

It is one thing for scholars and museum professionals to claim that a particular exhibition is innovative; it is quite another for visitors to do so. To include the visitors' perspectives requires consideration of who they were and how they actually saw the exhibition. How did the intended audience compare to the actual audience? How did visitors experience the exhibition? What did its design communicate? Did *We the People* give visitors a new perspective on the founding period? CHS did not engage in formative or summative evaluation of this exhibition and did not place comment books in the gallery to record visitors' responses. The discussion is thus by necessity based on observations; on interviews with educators, volunteer interpreters, and guards; and on survey research conducted by the author between January and April 1996. Although these surveys were not a random or representative sample, combined with interviews and observational research, they provide valuable information about visitors' impressions of *We the People*.

Aware that it was impossible to serve the whole of CHS's vast constituency at once, the exhibition team aimed for an audience with basic knowledge about the thirteen colonies, the war, and the process by which the Constitution was ratified.[9] Careful attention to the physical layout of the exhibition, however, provides a more accurate profile of the actual visitor. The artifacts and exhibition cases were installed to accommodate adults of average height. Not surprisingly, young children and visitors in wheelchairs found it uninviting. For conservation reasons the lighting level was quite low. The label copy was difficult to read because much of it was in 16–18 point type. Elderly visitors frequently bypassed the object labels because the print was too small. One woman who had forgotten her eyeglasses simply left the gallery. But this problem is not age specific. A twenty-eight-year-old visitor wrote: "Larger print on small signs would be appreciated."[10] The physical layout of the exhibition did not provide much room for people to gather. Volunteer interpreters, for this reason, often encouraged larger groups to proceed directly to *A House Divided: America in the Age of Lincoln.*

In light of these problems, it is important to determine who did not have access to *We the People.* Were Braille, large print, and foreign language labels available? Were the artifacts and labels adjusted for visitors with sight lines under four feet? Did the exhibition appeal to different learning styles? Was there anywhere to sit down? Was the lighting adequate? The answer to most of these questions was no, so what accounts for the popularity of this exhibition among visitors of all ages? While the designers and curators deserved much of the credit for its success, the artifacts themselves were a big draw. Many of the survey respondents were struck by the presence of the original documents. First-time visitors were often surprised to find such a sophisticated exhibition on early American history in Chicago. Some visitors returned to see artifacts they had missed during their previous visit.

What kind of visitor did *We the People* attract? For comparative purposes, it makes sense to begin by describing what kind of visitor CHS attracted in the late 1980s. These statistics are based on two studies conducted in June 1988 by the Leo Burnett Company, for CHS, and a third study conducted by the Metro Chicago Information Center in October 1995, which focused specifically on tourism, for Museums in the Park—an umbrella organization representing the Adler Planetarium, the Art Institute, the Chicago Academy of Sciences and Nature Museum, the Chicago Historical Society, the Field Museum, the Museum of Science and Industry, and the Shedd Aquarium. For the most part, CHS visitors in this period were between twenty-five and forty-four years of age, had lived in Chicago for at least five years, had obtained college or postgraduate degrees (77 percent), and earned about fifty thousand dollars a year. CHS members were older (from thirty-five to sixty-five), had lived in Chicago for over ten years, had obtained college or postgraduate degrees (78 percent), and occupied a slightly higher income bracket than the average visitor. In general, CHS attracted tourists with similar characteristics: they were predominately between thirty-one and forty years old, and their incomes averaged forty thousand dollars per year.[11] *We the People* visitors fit this same profile: they were white, nearly thirty-five years old, and had college degrees. Unlike CHS in general, *We the People* did not attract families with children under ten or with teenagers. Public high school students were the one exception. Many Chicago-area history teachers used the exhibition to supplement their course materials, so at any given time the gallery was filled with eleventh graders trying to complete assigned worksheets.

It took at least two hours to read the labels and view the objects in the exhibition, but the volunteer interpreters and security guards estimated that visitors spent about half an hour in the gallery. Several factors mitigated against a longer stay. The visitor surveys indicated that *We the People* was seldom the first exhibition on the visitor's itinerary because of its location in the west wing on the second floor.[12] Most visitors wrote that it was the second exhibition they visited, and for some it was the third or fourth. So museum fatigue might partially explain the brief stay. Longtime interpreter Nancy Wilson offered some possible explanations: the eighteenth- and early-nineteenth-century manuscripts were hard to read because they were faded, and perhaps the use of the English *f* in place of an *s* in the print documents made them difficult to understand.[13] The security guards, the group with the most direct and sustained contact with the public, mentioned that lighting was a frequent complaint. Some labels were obscured by the artifacts' shadows (in the case of the paintings); other labels were placed in corners where the lighting was too dim for visitors to read them. To complicate matters, the motion sensors turned off the lights if visitors stood still for too long. Finally, by the time visitors reached the "Constitution, Bill of Rights, 1781–91" section, they could hear the video introducing *A House Divided* in the adjacent exhibition. Tired, seduced by the opportunity to sit down, some visitors simply skipped the last three rooms of *We the People* and proceeded directly to the next exhibition.

If the average stay in *We the People* was thirty minutes, what kind of exhibition was it for visitors? Time is not necessarily a good indicator of a visitor's ability to grasp the theme of an exhibition. Education, frame of mind, and familiarity with the topic are all relevant factors. Even so, it is difficult to ignore that the real meat of the exhibition was contained in the labels, and these labels did not have much to recommend them. How a label looks is as important as what it says. Small print, awkward placement, disinterested tone, and dim lighting made the *We the People* labels uninviting. Although most research in museums shows that visitors only spend a few seconds reading a particular label, these statistics are misleading. Instead, visitors should be divided into those who read the labels and those who do not.[14] Those who do read labels spend about forty-five seconds viewing an artifact-label cluster. They prefer short sentences (eighteen to twenty words), large type, and lines that do not exceed sixty-five characters.[15]

Although the *We the People* labels generally conformed to this standard, some were difficult to read comfortably while standing. The label introducing the section on the "Constitution, Bill of Rights, 1781–91" was almost three hundred words long. Others, as Ellsworth Brown pointed out, were awkwardly placed. He went so far as to take a camera into the gallery to take a photo of a visitor kneeling on the floor with his head tipped back, in order

The 1868 Building—This architectural drawing represents the society's first building.

Remains of the 1868 Building—On October 9, 1871, the Chicago fire destroyed the society's building once advertised as a "perfectly fire proof structure."

The 1877 Building—Intended as a temporary structure, this building on the northwest corner of Ontario and Dearborn housed CHS from 1877 until 1892.

The 1896 Building—In 1896 the members opened a third building on the corner of Dearborn and Ontario streets and welcomed the public for the first time. In addition to Chicago, the exhibitions focused on American history, from the colonial period to the Civil War.

Charles F. Gunther—The society's largest acquisition of early American materials came from the estate of Charles F. Gunther.

Lincoln Park, 1932—Lacking the space or staff to properly care for the expanding collection, CHS opened a new building with library and museum facilities at the south end of Lincoln Park.

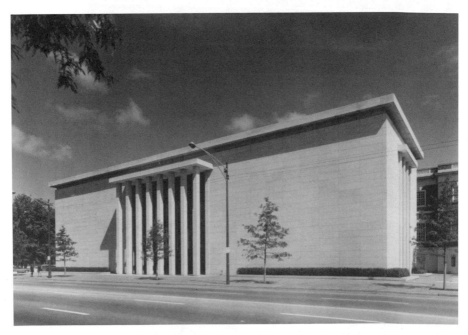

The 1972 Building—Voted the ugliest building in Chicago, the three-story addition provided space to experiment with new exhibitions.

The 1988 Building—CHS's most recent expansion enveloped the 1972 limestone building and added gallery, storage, laboratory, and work space as well as an underground storage vault to house manuscripts and architectural records.

Exhibiting the Civil War, 1911—On the fiftieth anniversary of the beginning of the Civil War, CHS hosted an exhibition of wartime memorabilia. Since its founding, CHS has organized at least a dozen Civil War-related exhibitions. The emphasis on military aspects continued until the 1970s.

Victorian Room—Featuring furniture from the Robert Hall McCormack House, the Victorian Room was one of the many period rooms that opened with the 1932 building. Volunteers frequently gave formal concerts to CHS visitors.

Paul Revere Room—The exhibitions that opened with the 1932 building paid homage to the heroes of American history, using two new interpretive techniques: dioramas and period rooms. Here is a reproduction of the master bedroom of Paul Revere's house in Boston, built around 1680.

Cover, First Issue—CHS director Paul Angle issued the society's first quarterly publication, *Chicago History*, in 1945, with hopes of attracting new members and disseminating scholarship about the city's history.

CHICAGO HISTORY

Citizens of
CHICAGO,
LOOK AT THIS!!

The Administration has SUSPENDED the improvement of your HARBOR. Two weeks' more work would open it to all kinds of Craft. Van Buren says he will "follow in the footsteps" of the present Executive. So, if he is elected, our Harbor may NEVER be completed, and the interest of the WHOLE WEST will doubtless be treated with scorn and contempt. *Merchants, Mechanics* and *Laborers*, will you endure this?

Broadside, 1836

Published Quarterly by the
CHICAGO HISTORICAL SOCIETY
VOLUME I   FALL, 1945   NUMBER 1

***Pioneer Life Gallery,* 1973**—Modeled after Old Sturbridge Village, *Pioneer Life* dramatized rural life before the Civil War. Volunteers demonstrated carding, spinning, dyeing, weaving, candle dipping, and corn shucking.

Lincoln Gallery, **1973**—This exhibit featured letters, personal memorabilia, furniture, paintings, the refurbished Lincoln dioramas, and a life-size replica of Lincoln's log cabin.

Native American Protest—In 1973 a group of Native American activists protested the racist stereotyping of the Fort Dearborn Massacre statue. In the forty years since, CHS has focused on documenting and interpreting the history of previously marginalized groups.

Chicago History Galleries—Harold Skramstad joined CHS as director in 1974 and focused the society's energy on Chicago-themed exhibitions such as the *Chicago History Galleries,* which opened in 1979.

We the People—Opened on September 12, 1987, *We the People: Creating a New Nation, 1765–1820* was one of the few bicentennial exhibitions offering a new perspective on the founding period. At the same time, this inventive exhibition brought about significant changes within the CHS.

A House Divided—Opened in 1990, *A House Divided: America in the Age of Lincoln* was the most ambitious Civil War exhibition CHS had ever mounted. It was also the first exhibition divided into sections with specific learning objectives.

A City Comes of Age: Chicago in the 1890s—This exhibit, which opened in 1990, featured the story of the Chicago stockyards.

"Voices from History"—The *A City Comes of Age: Chicago in the 1890s* team experimented with hiring actors dressed as historic figures to present dramatic monologues. This technique proved so successful that CHS included "Voices from History" in subsequent exhibitions.

Chicago Goes to War, 1941–1945—This exhibit, on view from 1992 to 1993, encouraged collaboration with local residents to collect twentieth-century artifacts.

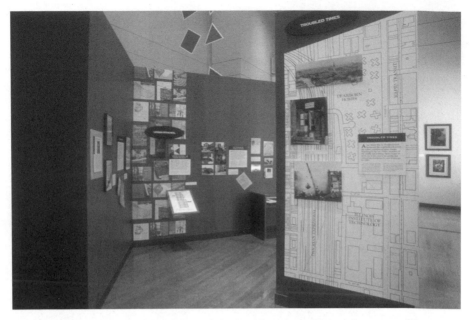

Douglas/Grand Boulevard: The Past and the Promise—An ambitious four-part exhibition series funded largely by the Joyce Foundation, *Neighborhoods: Keepers of Culture* was the first exhibition to formalize collaborations with community partners and re-examine assumptions about interpretive authority.

Neighborhood Interactives—Hands-on interactive exhibition components, intended for children under eleven, became popular components of the *Neighborhoods* project.

to show the staff that the labels were too small and positioned too low.[16] The labels' disinterested tone was a problem; to vary the presentation of material, the curators might have included excerpts from letters, speeches, or songs, which would have given visitors an opportunity to connect with the historical actors on a more personal level. The curators might also have written multitiered labels to appeal to different audiences. The first layer could contain the most important information for a simple cursory glance, the second could give more description, the third could provide the most dedicated readers with contextual information and analysis.[17] By giving a menu from which to choose, multitiered labeling might appeal to those who typically bypass the written text.

What, then, was the experience for visitors simply looking at the objects? As with all exhibitions, display techniques give visual cues. The size and placement of artifacts as well as the length of their labels indicate their importance. The most traditional artifacts in *We the People*—the Constitution, the Declaration of Independence, and the clothing worn by Washington and Adams—occupied more square footage than other artifacts and were accompanied by the largest labels. They were also sequestered in large climate-controlled cases, which gave them a visual importance that was difficult to ignore. Lighting helped visitors navigate the visual landscape. As visitors approached big-ticket items, the lights came up automatically. Intended as a conservation measure, this distracted viewers' attention away from the less conventional items, which was not difficult to do since the artifacts related to ordinary people tended to be smaller and less visually interesting. They were also more likely to be grouped with other artifacts and accompanied by smaller labels. One visitor wrote: "I would highlight some more of the 'lesser' known facts because if you only see the exhibit once, you may miss some excellent points [because of the] smaller print."[18] In this context, visitors who did not read the subsidiary text were presented with a relatively uncomplicated view of the past: the great documents were surrounded by portraits of the founders and heroic images of the war, whereas some of the most compelling objects—Hannah the Weaver's note (under five inches square), James Pike's powder horn (about fourteen inches long), and David Kennison's tea box (with no side longer than five inches)—simply could not compete.

The visual text of an exhibition is as important as the written text. The exhibition team consciously sought a traditional look, to be evocative of the late eighteenth and early nineteenth centuries. Young hoped to encourage people to reevaluate their knowledge of the period without making his interpretation too iconoclastic. The revisionist interpretation was thus cloaked in a conventional design.[19] To achieve this, Staples and Charles carpeted the gallery, lowered the ceilings, painted the walls federal blue, and installed a low-wattage lighting system. The cherry-wood cases and matching baseboards gave the exhibition a dignified but not aristocratic look, suggesting permanence and authority. Unlike the temporary exhibitions that were fitted into existing galleries, the west wing of the American history gallery was built to house *We the People*. The colors and the wood were chosen to complement the objects, and the dim lighting helped create an intimate, almost sacred, space. The exhibition team elected not to use marble because they thought it would be too reverential, but the lighting created the same effect. As visitors entered the gallery, their behavior changed; they lowered their voices and walked more slowly as if they had entered a church, a library, or a courthouse.

The conventional design attracted visitors, but it occasionally also buried the curators' innovative interpretation. When answering one of the survey questions, "Is it important to know who curated this exhibition?" one respondent wrote: "Not in this case since the approach is fairly traditional. If a new or atypical view was represented, it might be interesting to know the name." Young agreed that the design worked against the notion of a society in conflict.[20] The artifacts that illustrated competing notions of how best to govern the new nation were not highlighted, giving the false impression of consensus. In the section "Constitution, Bill of Rights, 1781–91," the bitter battles between Federalists and Anti-Federalists were reduced to one small case. To some degree this problem was beyond the team's control. In "The Republic Moves West," the curators wanted to highlight how westward expansion displaced Native Americans, but they could not locate enough artifacts to communicate the tragedy, for example. Yet, even in other sections where the artifacts were available, the contrast was not made sharply enough. In "Declaring Independence, 1776," the title page of John Adams's *Thoughts on Government* was silk-screened onto a label about Thomas Paine, but it was often mistaken for another version of *Common Sense* because Staples and Charles elected not to enlarge the reproduction.

These problems did not prevent some visitors from recognizing that *We the People* was telling a story they had not heard before, however. Over 35 percent of the survey respondents mentioned individuals or groups who had been marginalized within the historical record (soldiers, Native Americans, African Americans, immigrants, and women).[21] The following is a sample of responses to the question "Did you learn anything about the Revolutionary period that you did not know?"

I liked the emphasis on women's participation during the Revolutionary period.

it was interesting to see the period through the eyes of others, through Indians, etc.

I learned that the Indians allied themselves with the British government.

I learned about different historical figures—women and minorities—Mercy Otis Warren, Phillis Wheatley.

James Pike carved into his powder horn the convictions of the New England militia.
the [number] of slaves and indentured servants.

[The exhibit] pulled together the stories from many perspectives (men, women, native,
black).

Yes, European involvement in the war as well as women and [I]ndians.

Learned more about Phillis Wheatley about whom I knew very little. Also, I had never
heard of Paul Cuffee. As I now teach all African American high school students I am
focusing on areas that are more meaningful to them.

Yes, that several thousand blacks fought in the Revolution . . . that thousands escaped
slavery during the war.[22]

In spite of the conventional design, a significant proportion of the visitors in
1996 applauded the unconventional focus on race, gender, ethnicity, and class.
    Although the exhibition team assumed that visitors come to museums to
see themselves, this did not seem to be the case. When asked "Is there anything that you didn't agree with or that you would like to see changed, omitted, or added?" one fifty-year-old German woman answered: "More on
African Americans." A twenty-six-year-old white woman requested: "More
emphasis should be placed on the unwillingness of the founders to confront
slavery."[23] These answers are revealing for museums, which believe that multicultural exhibitions appeal to multicultural audiences. Terry Fife explained
that this simply was not true:

What I came to understand as a practicing historian is that people are not literal in
seeing themselves in history, it's such a personal and subjective experience and the interaction is still virtually unknown and largely undefined even by historians who do
it. . . . It's often reduced to such a simple formula where it's clearly a one-way street.
Here you are a certain kind of person with certain kinds of stripes and polka dots. Let's
show you something of your stripes and polka dots and you'll be interested in history.
Since we don't know how people become interested in history it's so presumptuous of
us to assume that that's the way to do it.[24]

    This is not to say that female visitors were not inspired by the life of
Deborah Sampson or that Paul Cuffee did not serve as a role model for
African Americans, but audiences of all ages, genders, races, and classes

were attracted to different things. It is not enough to assume that who you are is a good indicator of what you will find interesting.

It might seem ironic that an exhibition that raised questions about the limitations of the founders' vision could have gained so much support in 1987. Donors did not withdraw funding for what was ostensibly a multicultural exhibition; CHS trustees did not seem concerned that the interpretation was too radical; and, with few exceptions, visitors and scholars praised the focus on populations that have been marginalized from the historical record. Much of the exhibition's success was the result of the team's sensitivity to the exhibition as a medium of communication. Young and Fife realized that mounting an exhibition required balancing celebration and analysis. Staples and Charles paid careful attention to the visual message of the exhibition and created a nonthreatening physical environment. Instead of feeling uninformed or stupid, visitors left *We the People* with the sense that the Revolutionary period was far more interesting than they had remembered.

The exhibition became the center of a web of interrelated changes, which positioned CHS as one of the nation's premier urban history museums. Its most immediate legacy was to act as a model for the staff planning the next permanent exhibition, *A House Divided*, which opened in January 1990. But *We the People* had a more lasting impact. While Mary Janzen was correct in her assessment that it should not "be measured by the strengths and weaknesses of one exhibit alone, but in the impact it has had on the institution as a whole," its influence was more far-reaching than the exhibition team, or CHS, could have anticipated.[25] With the possible exception of the Neighborhoods project, *We the People* was one of the society's most innovative exhibitions in recent memory. It functioned as a catalyst for change because, even though it came from outside the institution, it managed to alter the internal culture. The team's status as outsiders posed some problems, especially for Fife, but it also encouraged CHS staff to reevaluate their relationship to their collections, their constituencies, and the academic world.

When asked how *We the People* affected the institution, the staff overwhelmingly mentioned the use of Alfred Young and the consulting scholars. Although Perry Duis had functioned as project historian for *Chicago: Creating New Traditions* (1976), Young and Fife were the first academic historians to serve as curators for an exhibition. Although art museums have employed art historians as curators for decades, in the 1980s this was a relatively new practice for history museums, which might explain why history curators were so reluctant to share their authority. For many years these curators held elite positions within their institutions, and educators, designers, publication staffs, and docents were clearly subordinated to them. Seen as authorities in their fields, they were given authority to collect and interpret as they saw fit. The formation of the NEH and its insistence on the use of university scholars brought about some significant changes.[26] Although the NEH mentioned skill and experience as important criteria, professional standards largely meant academic achievement. When the CHS curators were measured against the NEH standard, they lacked the necessary academic credentials. Aware that the exhibition program could not survive without these important federal funds, Ellsworth Brown decided to turn to academic scholars for assistance.

His decision was also motivated by an awareness that the financial health of the institution was contingent upon the staff's ability to respond to the public's needs. The demographic changes in Chicago since the 1960s had profoundly altered the profile of the museum's audience and supporters. No longer able to rely upon the generosity of a few elite donors, CHS found itself beholden to constituencies representing diverse interests and social groups. In this context relevancy was akin to survival. An awareness of the market, though, should not minimize Brown's commitment to making the institution's interpretive programs more inclusive. A historian whose own research focused on Native Americans, Brown firmly believed that social history was the vehicle to make the stories of marginalized groups accessible to diverse audiences. Outside historians such as Young and Fife were given authority over the interpretive process that had formerly been reserved for curators because none of the CHS curators had the requisite training.

Brown's unilateral decision to support *We the People* indicated that CHS curators no longer had control over the exhibition schedule either. In the past a curator would bring an idea for an exhibition directly to the director, and together they would iron out the details. For *We the People,* Brown proposed the idea, gave Janzen the authority to recruit the team, and made no effort to include the in-house curators in the process. The presence of Young and Fife implied that CHS curators were not real historians. One curator complained that the exhibition team treated the in-house curators as "Stepin' Fetchits"—collections managers "who got out the goods."[27] Another curator was reported to have said: "Why do we have to have these damn historians telling us what to do?" A third complained that the exhibition team intruded upon "their" collection.[28]

Partly the result of personality clashes, these complaints also reflected different philosophical approaches to historical interpretation. The CHS curators had pioneered methods of making history accessible and useful to a wide range of CHS's constituencies over the years, but they were not given much of the credit. Throughout the planning of *We the People,* the in-house curators complained that their expertise was devalued and that they were being treated by Brown and the exhibition team as antiquarians instead of as professionals. In a letter to development director Marc Hilton concerning the Fry Foundation's staff enrichment program, Young betrayed this subtle bias.[29] His letter implied that curators were parochial and uninformed; the creative dialogue he mentioned regarding the exhibition team positioned the historian as teacher and curator as student.

The use of outside historians came at a time when curators everywhere were working to professionalize their occupation. In the 1970s and early 1980s the pages of the most prestigious museum periodical in the United States, *Museum News,* were filled with articles debating how to legitimize museum work.[30] Yet careful analysis revealed that the structure and culture of museums functioned as impediments to full professional status. The sheer diversity of museums and the skills required to maintain them meant that art, science, and history museums could not agree on how best to educate and regulate their employees.[31] Lack of autonomy also posed a problem. Trustees and directors as a rule rarely consulted the museum staff about their fiduciary or administrative control of the museum. The AAM regularly addressed issues ranging from accreditation to staff relations, but thousands of museums in this country did not subscribe to these standards. It is in this context that CHS shifted interpretive authority from the in-house curators to the *We the People* team.

Whatever the CHS staff's relationship with Young, Fife, Staples, and Charles, Young and Fife remained outsiders, removed from the daily operations of the institution. The issues raised by *We the People* made it clear to Ellsworth Brown that the process by which exhibitions were selected and organized needed revision, and the resulting changes had a profound impact on claims to interpretive authority. *We the People* was the first time that an exhibition team had been directed by a project coordinator; instead of giving the curator the responsibility for staffing and budget decisions, Brown appointed Mary Janzen to serve in that capacity. Janzen's presence indicated that CHS was willing to accept a new kind of authority, based on administrative, not interpretive, expertise. Because of Janzen's success, Brown decided to make project coordinators a permanent feature of the exhibition program. Late in 1986 he hired Susan Tillett to serve as the institution's first director of curatorial affairs, thus formalizing team-based projects and visitor advocacy.

As with any paradigm shift, a new generation of practitioners must replace the old before change can become institutionalized. Staff members who did not agree with these policy changes or did not measure up to the new professional standards either were encouraged to leave or left of their own volition. Ellsworth Brown offered early retirement to several longtime staff members; curator of paintings Joseph Zwyicki, registrar Teresa Krutz, associate librarian Grant Dean, and general services administrator Tom Watson accepted. Realizing she would never again have the freedom or support to mount exhibitions of her own choosing, curator of decorative arts Sharon Darling left in 1986 to become director of the newly organized Motorola Museum. Olivia Mahoney served as the interim department head until Robert Goler was hired in 1988. Wendy Greenhouse became the institution's first professional curator of painting and sculpture. In 1989 Elizabeth Jachimow-icz was pressured to resign and was eventually replaced by her assistant, Su-san Samek, who had recently completed an MFA at the Art Institute of Chicago. For the most part these new curators were academically trained and supportive of the new institutional structure.

We the People also required that CHS staff rethink the meaning of the ob-jects in their collection. Instead of building a historical argument around a collection, Young and Fife utilized a story line or thematic approach. Arti-facts were important not for their physical properties but because of the story they told. The Liverpool pitchers painted with speeches or slogans had been on display for years at CHS as the skillful creations of colonial craftsmen, but for Young and Fife they became evidence that household items were highly politicized. The exhibition was filled with such creative interpretations, but this approach was not universally applauded. One curator, reflecting on the experience, explained: "All hints of connoisseurship and expertise, of passion for objects and artifacts just disappeared totally. It became a way of bringing in outside historians who essentially put their book on the wall. I really feel strongly that that was a huge mistake." The focus shifted away from the ob-ject and onto the label because objects were assumed to be incapable of telling their own stories. Director of publications and editor Russell Lewis ar-gued in the 1986–1987 annual report that "most artifacts don't speak for themselves. It's up to the curators to give them meaning, and they do that through juxtaposition, context, relationships."[32]

The new precedence given to the narrative changed the selection process of artifacts. Instead of building an exhibition around a collection of similar materials, Young and Fife chose artifacts because they fit into various the-matic categories, but this approach had its limitations. CHS did not have enough materials to support their interpretive framework. If the artifacts re-lating to men who held public office, fought battles, and published writings were plentiful and well cataloged, artifacts that told a more inclusive story were practically invisible. A thematic approach also necessitated heavy re-liance upon written text. Since the connections between a Dutch tulip chest from 1660 and a ceramic figurine of the Madonna and child from 1750 were not immediately obvious to visitors, the curators depended upon labels to tell their story.

We the People changed how the institution assigned interpretive responsi-bility. Late in July 1987 Young and Fife became concerned that they were not going to get credit for their work on the exhibition. Unaware that crediting curators was not a common practice in museums, Young wrote to Gary Kulick at the Smithsonian for advice. When Kulick explained that the Smithsonian did not have an attribution policy, Young decided to take up the issue with Ellsworth Brown. In a letter to Brown he explained that the omissions of acknowledgment "suggest a pattern of inexperience in dealing with professional historians as curators, a failure to acknowledge what the historical profession would consider as authorship."[33] Young argued that the scholarship for *We the People* was equivalent to the work he would put into a book. Just as he expected his name to appear on the book's cover, he also expected a credit panel to appear at the beginning of *We the People*. Sympathetic to Young's argument and aware that such a policy would be another opportunity to showcase CHS exhibitions as scholarly enterprises, Brown drafted an attribution policy that is still in effect at the institution. From the museum's perspective, the new policy helped demonstrate that exhibitions, like all cultural productions, are the result of certain perspectives.

The visitors barely noticed, however. Of the seventy-six survey respondents who replied to the question "Is it important to you to know who curated the exhibition?" twenty-four (31%) answered yes, but only one identified Young and Fife as the curators. Of the twenty-four, those who identified themselves as teachers or students seemed more willing to question the curators' interpretation and expressed some awareness that history is not simply a recitation of facts:

I don't know who curated the exhibit, but since history is subjective, it would help us to understand the bias of the exhibit if we knew who the curator was.

Yes, if you are looking to understand why the curator chose to include/not include certain facts/perspectives/stories.

It would be interesting to know since I believe all history is interpretive and political.[34]

But the majority of the respondents who answered the question did not challenge the curators' perspective or authority. One respondent answered: "No, because I trust a source in a museum." Another explained: "No. I just like to learn the information. As long as it's true, I don't care who gives it to me."[35] Although few were quite as trusting, the responses implied that whereas academics or teachers might be interested in such things, the visitors were not; subverting the authoritarian voice of the museum was not a priority. The visitors came to the museum expecting a temple, not a forum.

Understanding how museums function in public discourse might explain why. Museums have, for years, cultivated their image as institutions that people respected without always being sure as to why.[36] Familiar with this convention, most visitors come to history museums not to raise questions about the past but to learn what happened. Unlike academic historians who continually raise questions about objectivity and truth, museums have jealously guarded their interpretive authority. While Young and Fife occasionally presented dissenting voices and admitted that their interpretation was incomplete, the conventional design works against this approach.

If the exhibition failed to qualify the curators' interpretation, *We the People: Voices and Images of a New Nation,* the companion volume published in 1993, was more successful. Aware that readers were curious about how artifacts were selected and identified, Young and Fife invented a section called the "Historian's Voice." Set off from the main narrative, these side bars raised philosophical questions about historical research: "History by Association" discussed the problems faced by the *We the People* team when conducting original research on ordinary people; "The Declaration as History and as Icon" talked about what constituted an authentic object. Because few readers had a sense of how historians practice their craft, Young and Fife used these sections to pique interest in the historical process and to prove that interpretations were always educated guesses. The addition of the "Historian's Voice" also signaled an important change in the relationship between the curator and the reader. Instead of an authoritarian figure, the curator became an interpreter.

By exposing the historical process to public scrutiny, Young and Fife invited readers to accept or reject their interpretation. This was made explicit in the final sentence of the book's introduction: "Readers may disagree with our conclusions. Indeed the original sources in this book are an invitation to readers to draw their own conclusions."[37] The book was more open to debate and discussion than the exhibition, although it never fully abandoned the voice of authority. It did, however, make it clear that the exhibition is *a* story about the past, not *the* story. In the end the book's approach had more lasting value. In addition to presenting specific information about the Revolutionary period, Young and Fife actually provided readers with the tools to engage in historical analysis.

Young's efforts to bring academic standards into the museum also changed the value placed on exhibitions by the CHS staff. Exhibitions tend to be temporary enterprises and are seldom seen as legitimate contributions to historical scholarship. Until the NEH in the 1980s required that museums archive materials related to exhibition production, CHS staff had treated them as disposable products, not artifacts in and of themselves. Those exhibitions that did not generate a catalog were not seen as important contributions to knowledge. When Young introduced the prospect of outside reviews, the institution's attitude toward the exhibition program changed markedly. To accommodate reviewers and the public, Young asked Russell Lewis to prepare the narrative and descriptive labels and an object checklist. CHS began requiring that curators and project managers submit their files to the archives and manuscripts department. This was the first time that CHS had made these kinds of materials available to the public. Both policies signaled an awareness that exhibitions provide an important opportunity to document the institution's interpretive activities.

The success of *We the People* also helped convince other scholars to become involved in curating history exhibitions. Eric Foner argued that Young was instrumental in his decision to become the co-curator with Olivia Mahoney of CHS's Civil War exhibition, *A House Divided*. Foner consulted Terry Fife about logistical concerns and was especially interested in finding out how she and Young had divided the labor.[38] When Gary Nash was asked by the Historical Society of Pennsylvania to serve as the curator for *Finding Philadelphia's Past: Visions and Revisions* in 1988, he turned to Young for advice. While he was considering whether to accept the commission, he visited *We the People* for ideas and became very enthusiastic about the possibility of communicating to a larger audience. In this context *We the People* became a tangible way to recruit academic historians into the museum field.

The exhibition's most enduring legacy was as a model for other history museums. The NEH between 1985 and 1989 handed out copies of the second implementation proposal, as a sample grant for applicants in search of federal funding. Marsha Semmel, program officer in the division of public programs at NEH, estimated that her office distributed the *We the People* proposal to over forty museums.[39] As a result museum professionals from around the country solicited advice from Young and Fife and in some cases visited the installation. Throughout 1985 and 1986, before the exhibition opened to the public, co-curators of *Finding Philadelphia's Past* Elizabeth Jarvis and David Cassedy reviewed the exhibition script and grant applications and consulted Fife.[40] Gary Nash asked Young to comment on their script, because of the similarities between the topics. In 1988 Karen Gering brought a team of curators to CHS from the Missouri Historical Society in order to view *We the People* and gather ideas for their new municipal exhibition.[41] When the NMAH decided to revise sections of *After the Revolution* in 1989, Barbara Clark Smith invited Young to serve as a consultant for the Philadelphia section. After several on-site visits, Young reviewed and commented on revised versions of the script and helped the NMAH team revise the artisan installation.

The success of *We the People* also proved that CHS's constituencies were more than willing to embrace complex historical interpretations, demonstrating that CHS staff could not only withstand but even benefit from change. Although many of these issues had been discussed or attempted prior to 1987, *We the People* became the crucible in which series of changes were successfully implemented. To argue that a single exhibition functioned as a catalyst requires careful attention, however, to the degree to which those changes have been institutionalized. During the transition years 1987–1993, CHS created a new management structure, built a new addition, rewrote the mission statement, renewed its commitment to urban history through a series of biennial exhibitions, and expanded the reach of the education department. In order to determine what counts as change, it is important to make distinctions between innovation, defined as temporary strategies in response to or in anticipation of a particular demand and often intended to avoid controversy, and change, defined as interventions that disrupt categories of knowledge without simply reinforcing the current power structure. Evaluating whether *We the People* produced institutional change requires careful attention to what happened afterward.

CHAPTER FOUR

The Transition Years,

1987–1993

We had evolved from simply being a collector of history,
or "Chicago's attic," to an institution on a journey
to reach out to the city's diverse groups.
—CHS BOARD CHAIRMAN RICHARD NEEDHAM,
ANNUAL REPORT (1991–1992)

The 1980s and early 1990s was a time of crisis for American museums. Just as museums began to express a new eagerness to update exhibitions and public programs so as to reflect new scholarship and growing cultural diversity, they were criticized by conservative politicians and academics for rejecting traditional American values.[1] The most visible manifestation of this struggle involved funding from the NEA and NEH. The National Foundation on the Arts and Humanities Act of 1965 (Public Law 89-209) held that "in the administration of this act there be given the fullest attention to freedom of artistic and humanistic expression." For the next two decades legislators were largely removed from guiding the direction of the agencies. This changed in 1985 when Richard Armey (R-Texas) tried to eliminate the NEA because it funded "gay-oriented literary journals."[2] Armey's attack, justified as a matter of judgment and values, positioned the arts and humanities as a new political battlefield. This and subsequent controversies (see the introduction) provoked a series of battles over public funding. Declaring that tax dollars should not support obscenity or leftist historical revisionism, Senators Jesse Helms (R-North Carolina), Alphonse D'Amato (R-New York), John Danforth (R-Missouri), Ted Stevens (R-Alaska), and Representatives Dana Rohrabacher (R-California) and Armey fought to place restrictions on the use of federal money, which had already been cut under the Reagan administration.

The resulting budget cuts and Public Law 101-121, which denied federal funds to indecent projects, reduced the number of programs that would otherwise have qualified for funding and forever changed the course of federal support.

While less ideologically based, the funding situation at the state and local level contributed to the overall sense of crisis. In January 1993 the New-York Historical Society took a $1.5 million loan in exchange for $3 million collateral from Sotheby's auction house.[3] In spite of this unorthodox and controversial strategy, a month later the society temporarily closed to the public, after 189 years of continuous operation. In that same year the state of Illinois cut state appropriations for museums that had once totaled $3 million per year.[4] Corporate support was not immune from these trends; overall giving to the arts and humanities declined from $7.5 billion in 1987 to $6.1 billion in 1994.[5] Not only offering fewer gifts, corporations also changed their giving patterns and began concentrating money in areas where they had a direct influence and became more reluctant to fund innovative projects. While foundations continued to fund programs aimed at diverse audiences, even they began imposing stricter rules on their grantees.

The funding crisis was compounded by dramatic decreases in paid admissions. Museum attendance in the United States, which had been steady for most of the century, fell in the early 1990s.[6] In 1992–1993 in Chicago, the Adler Planetarium, the Shedd Aquarium, and the Museum of Science and Industry reported reductions of 17–25 percent in their overall attendance. Even the Henry Ford Museum and Greenfield Village and Colonial Williamsburg, two institutions that have for the past three decades attracted a steady stream of visitors, were seriously affected.[7] While museum professionals and industry analysts blamed the ailing tourist industry, demographic changes seem a more plausible explanation. The U.S. Census Bureau estimated that African American and Latino populations will continue to grow, and whites will eventually qualify as minorities in certain urban areas.[8] But for the most part museums continued to advertise and cater to white middle-class audiences, and several studies explain why. A 1989 survey conducted by the Pennsylvania Historical Museum Commission revealed that the average museum visitor was white and aged in the mid-forties. Black, Hispanic, and Asian visitors together constituted less than 10 percent of the total.[9] These findings were echoed in a similar study conducted in Los Angeles in 1990, which found that 93 percent of the city's museum visitors were white, even though the local population was 38 percent white, 36 percent Latino, 15 percent African American, and 12 percent Asian.[10] As whites continue to leave the cities, nonwhites—historically ignored by mainstream museums—had no incentive to make up the difference in museum attendance.

In this environment of reduced funding and declining admissions, CHS sought to reinvent itself. "For many years," *Chicago Tribune* columnist Jay

Pridmore argued, "polite society found a sweet home at the Chicago Historical Society. Its directors were the social lions of the community. . . . The museum was known for field trips, Lincoln's death bed and viewing history in the soft focus of the distant past."[11] In the late 1980s and early 1990s things began to change, however. Programs and exhibitions addressed race relations, class conflict, and labor strife, topics that had previously been considered too confrontational or controversial for funders and visitors. Population groups that CHS staff had labeled underrepresented started to participate in public programs in higher numbers. Three African Americans, a Hispanic, several women, and an urban historian were appointed to the board of trustees. Revisionist historians collaborated on exhibitions. Local residents donated objects and participated in oral history projects, and the words *diversity, accountability,* and *public service* appeared in institutional publications with increasing regularity. What accounts for this change? Reduced funding and declining admissions were important forces, but they were not the only factors.

Change in history museums was driven by professionals trained at Winterthur, Hagley, and Cooperstown, or in other programs that focused on social history. These new museum scholars were interested in urban history and community outreach. The new CHS management structure, the building program, the rewriting of the mission statement, the shift toward urban history, and the growing visibility of the education department were all precipitated by these new professionals, who shared one thing in common—a commitment to sharing authority with CHS's diverse constituencies.

Many of the innovations attempted in *We the People*—the thematic focus, the integration of different collections, collaborations with academic historians, and the use of project directors and project teams—became formalized with the hiring of Susan Tillett as CHS's first director of curatorial affairs in 1987. The impetus for the position came from CHS president and director Ellsworth Brown, who needed someone to manage the curatorial and collections staff while he guided the capital expansion. Tillett's hiring also reflected Brown's desire to redistribute interpretive authority among the staff and to encourage them to communicate more effectively.[12] Prior to Tillett's arrival the curators reported to the director and seldom proposed interdepartmental projects. Tillett instituted three major changes that had been suggested by the Scope Study consultants in 1982: she coordinated an in-house enrichment program; she formalized the team-centered approach; and she made urban history the focus of the interpretive programs. Each of these changes became an arena in which to question who owned history.

The staff enrichment program became Tillett's primary vehicle for generating internal change. In 1987 CHS received a sixty-thousand-dollar grant from the Lloyd A. Fry Foundation to establish a two-year program that would involve most of the interpretive staff. The program was divided into four parts: the establishment of a committee to develop and evaluate exhibitions, a course in Chicago history, workshops led by museum consultants, and site visits to other museums.[13] One of the unspoken goals of the staff enrichment program was to transform CHS from a group of independently functioning units into an institution committed to interdepartmental cooperation. It was not just a matter of efficiency but, rather, an issue of recognizing that what happens in the library, costumes collection, or education department has a profound impact on the institution's ability to serve its constituencies. This shift of the institution's operations core from collections management to public service reflected a significant shift in philosophy.

Teams became an important part of the transition. The team-centered approach grew out of the awareness that curators were not equipped to address the needs of the society's diverse constituencies because of their limited contact with the public. Although qualified to interpret objects and artifacts, curators represented only one part of the exhibition process. While CHS had used teams to organize the *Chicago History Galleries* and *We the People,* Tillett insisted that these teams become more inclusive. Project directors took over the primary financial and management responsibilities that had previously rested with curators. To meet the demands of funders and constituencies, CHS also began inviting academic historians to join the exhibition teams. Where CHS had once relied on historians as consultants (for *Chicago: Creating New Traditions* and the *Chicago History Galleries,* for example), in the late 1980s historians became curators in their own right. Tillett, like the Scope Study consultants, believed that thematic exhibitions utilizing social history as an interpretive perspective would appeal to larger and more diverse constituencies. Since few CHS curators were trained as social historians, academic scholars became necessary allies. Additionally, recognizing the communicative potential of museums, exhibition teams incorporated individuals with high levels of visitor contact in the decision-making process. In this context, visitor advocacy became a new kind of authority. The transition was, to borrow terminology from the business world, about valuing different skill centers. Although the curatorial skill center remained important, marketing, audience, and academic skill centers that had not been highly regarded or utilized in the past gained currency.[14]

Tillett's approach offered CHS something new. Prior to the 1980s museums had closely resembled academic institutions. The primary goal was the quest for and dissemination of knowledge by individual curators. Cuts in funding coupled with dwindling admission receipts forced museums to alter their emphasis. Instead of universities, museums came to resemble corporations, where different skills and talents were blended to create collaborative products.[15] The museum literature had only just begun to address organizational change, so professionals like Tillett turned to the private sector for guidance. From these sources Tillett borrowed two concepts, that of authority without influence and that of teamwork, which have since become the core of what has been labeled post-heroic leadership. Heroic leadership is characterized by a situation where a leader or manager is responsible for coordinating the activities of subordinates. The leader's job is to assume control. In contrast, post-heroic leadership is characterized by the sharing of responsibility. A post-heroic leader focuses on a common vision and works to build a strong team of individuals who act independently and thus feel ownership of projects.[16]

Tillett's understanding of post-heroic leadership was influenced in particular by the work of David Bradford, a professor of organizational behavior at the Stanford University Graduate School of Business. Bradford's most important contribution to the field of organizational leadership is the notion of influence without authority. This theory argues that successful leadership is contingent upon developing mutual influence in lieu of the formal exercise of authority. In this context, reciprocity is the key ingredient in all organizational transactions. Power, and by extension success, comes from the ability to meet the needs of others, not by controlling their behavior.[17]

Despite slight variations, the professional development literature on museums shares a common belief that interpretive decisions should be made by groups of professionals who have the skills, ability, and desire to complete a given task. The teamwork model is in direct contrast to a traditional hierarchy, where one person is in charge. Decentralized decision making, the core of team-based organizations, has the benefit of growth and empowerment.[18] Successful projects require that team members work interdependently toward a common goal and share accountability for success or failure. Responsibility and thus authority are shared. While teams may be led or directed, the power to make final decisions resides with the individual members.

Tillett's post-heroic management style, which shifted away from connoisseurship toward interdepartmental planning, heightened the ideological differences among the curatorial staff members. While some of the curators welcomed her presence, others felt she limited their decision-making authority. Complaints—that the proposed thematic exhibitions were boring, or that team projects would fail because educators, outside scholars, and project directors were not trained to care for and interpret the objects—obscured the real issue, which was a deeply felt resistance to change. Although Tillett recognized that this process had a very real human dimension, she did not allow staff resistance to overshadow the organization's needs.

The internal changes generated by the staff enrichment program did not become evident until the building renovation was complete. While the capital expansion program was originally intended to add an underground storage facility, Brown, the trustees, and the architects decided that CHS could afford to build a new facade to connect the 1932 building and 1972 addition. Ostensibly designed to accommodate the growth of the collections and staff, the addition also helped to coordinate the physical and intellectual environment of CHS. Although beautiful, the 1932 Georgian building, designed by Graham, Anderson, Probst, and White, more closely resembled a church or courthouse and was an imposing structure that intimidated visitors who might be unfamiliar with the society and its offerings. The lobby of the 1972 building was barren, and the facade, devoid of windows, failed to convey the impression that CHS was open to the public. A staff committee concluded in 1985 that the lack of signage and the Fort Dearborn Rescue monument, which had been the subject of protest by Native American activists in 1973, provided an unwelcoming first impression of the society.[19]

Aware that the physical environment influenced the museum experience, Brown, the trustees, and the architects worked to make the 1988 addition as inviting as possible. Instead of reproducing the imposing Georgian facade on the west side (Clark Street), architects Holabird and Root covered up the 1972 building and decorated the street-level entrance with aluminum-frame windows, steel trusses and cables, and colorful arcade windows. The east side (Lake Shore Drive) was redesigned as a spacious public plaza. The 1988 renovation reflected openness and accessibility by giving visitors the opportunity to look inside and see the lobby, restaurant, and store. The lobby was no longer a mere walkway but instead an informal exhibition space featuring sculpture, stained glass, and contemporary objects. An information kiosk equipped with a computer was available for visitor orientation, the coat-check room and bookstore were expanded, and the Big Shoulders Café was added.

Visitors are more comfortable in facilities that have bright, welcoming lobbies, adequate signage, and friendly staff members to greet them.[20] Every decision, from architectural design to the placement of security personnel, shapes the public's view of the institution. Taken as an artifact in itself, the 1972 building was a sealed box more interested in protecting the collections than in attracting new constituencies. The 1988 addition conveyed a very different message. The see-through construction demonstrated that CHS was a lively place worth visiting.

The process of planning and constructing the renovation encouraged CHS to rethink its purpose as well. Collecting, preserving, and interpreting the history of the city of Chicago, the state of Illinois, and selected areas of American history no longer constituted an adequate description of the institution's activities. With the assistance of Paul Krauss of the consulting firm of McKinsey and Company, Brown and the trustees decided they needed to revise the mission statement to guide the activities of the society. Rewriting the mission forced the staff and trustees to ask fundamental questions about the institution's purpose: Why does CHS exist? How can CHS best serve its varied constituencies? The revision reflected the recent turn toward multicultural-ism and collaboration and formalized a decade's worth of change. The fol-lowing revised mission was adopted in March 1989:

In fulfillment of its role as the historian of metropolitan Chicago and as a cultural in-stitution of long traditions, the Chicago Historical Society's mission is: 1. To interpret and present the history of Chicago to the city's diverse public groups through exhibi-tions, programs, and publications that educate and respond to their identified needs. 2. To collect and preserve a variety of objects and records related to Chicago. The col-lections will provide material to document the city's evolution, serve the research community, and educate the general public. To fulfill this mission, the Society will seek continuing help from scholars and other experts to define collecting strategies, to identify contemporary urban issues, and to develop interpretive programming. To en-gage a broad and highly qualified range of experts, the Society will commit resources to make its objects and documentary materials easily accessible. The Society will also pursue the related subjects of the United States to 1865 and the state of Illinois, to the extent that they place local history in larger contexts.[21]

Whereas the 1977 collecting statement and the 1984 "Statement of Collecting Scope" shifted the institution's focus to Chicago, the 1989 mission set forth the responsibility of the society to interpret and present a diverse history of the city. It also demonstrated that CHS's perspective on history had changed.

The trend toward focusing on the social needs of constituencies came partly in response to funders' requests for inclusiveness. In the 1980s and 1990s, despite the charged political climate, federal agencies and foundations became interested in sponsoring programs that targeted previously marginal-ized groups. The NEH and NEA, the Lila Wallace–Reader's Digest Fund, the MacArthur Foundation, the Joyce Foundation, and the Fry Foundation were all very active in promoting multicultural exhibitions and public programs. Not surprisingly, CHS was not the only institution to embark upon a more reflec-tive dialogue. Museums throughout the United States revised their statements of purpose to reflect contemporary society. In 1989 the Detroit Historical De-partment and Society changed their mission to emphasize their commitment to Detroit's rich multiethnic heritage.[22] In 1991 the Historical Society of Wash-ington, D.C., adopted a new mission statement, pledging "to use the past to enrich the life of today's Washington and to foster among its diverse commu-nities a strong sense of civic identity upon which to build a shared vision of the city's future."[23] Dozens of other institutions followed suit.

CHS's mission reflected a change in the institution's primary constituency. While the institution previously had directed its activities toward members, the new mission placed an emphasis on students, families with small chil-dren, scholars, senior citizens, and population groups that the staff had considered underrepresented, including African Americans, Latinos, and Asian Americans.[24] Instead of catering to members and donors, the new mission made the staff and trustees accountable to the community at large. This transition provoked a debate over the name of the institution. Worried that the word *society* implied an exclusive membership, several staff members recommended renaming it the Chicago Historical Museum or the Chicago Historical Resource Center to reflect the new emphasis on accessibility. CHS staff had good reason for concern. A 1988 report prepared for the Brooklyn Historical Society indicated that the local community (identified as nonusers of the institution) had no idea what a historical society was. Some guessed it was group of people who worked to save old buildings; none realized it was a museum that could be visited.[25] Although CHS administration decided to retain the name to avoid confusion with donors and funders, the debate signaled a new focus on the public.

Exhibitions and public programs became the most visible manifestation of the institution's new mission. *Profiles of Black Chicagoans* (February 1–July 9, 1989), *I Dream a World: Portraits of Black Women Who Changed America* (August 25–October 27, 1991), and *The Art of Archibald J. Motley, Jr.* (October 23, 1991–March 17, 1992) focused on African American history. *A House Divided: America in the Age of Lincoln* (a permanent exhibition that opened in January 1990), *A City Comes of Age: Chicago in the 1890s* (October 24, 1990–July 14, 1991), *Chicago Goes to War, 1941–1945* (May 24, 1992–August 15, 1993), and *Grand Illusions: Chicago's World's Fair of 1893* (May 1, 1993–July 17, 1994) all addressed how diverse groups shaped the history of the city and the nation. By addressing race, gender, ethnicity, and class, CHS offered constituencies new perspectives on history. The "Sojourner Program," "Cities-in-Schools," "Voices from History," and "Passports," all public programs sponsored by the education department, reflected greater interpretive diversity.

In conjunction with exhibitions and public programs, CHS began a new practice of soliciting visitors' opinions. Comment books were placed in selected galleries to encourage visitors to record their reactions to the exhibitions. To indicate the value of these comments to the institution, the 1988–1989 annual report published two responses to *The Whole World Is Watching: Inside and Outside the 1968 Democratic Convention* (August 15, 1988–January 15, 1989). In the concluding paragraph of an article on lighting and design in the March/April 1992 edition of the society's calendar of events, *Past Times,* CHS went so far as to invite criticism: "You can help shed light on these matters, too, by letting us know what works—and what doesn't —in our exhibitions. We welcome your comments. Don't keep us in the dark about how we can provide the very best museum experience for you."[26] Both *A City Comes of Age* and *Chicago Goes to War* asked visitors to write about problems and issues that they thought would be relevant to the city in the next century. What might seem a trivial gesture actually gave visitors a sense that their opinions were valued and their concerns were being addressed.

An urban history museum can be one of two things, either an institution that is merely situated in an urban environment or one that is dedicated to studying and interpreting this environment in all its diversity. For most of its lifetime, CHS was an American history museum that just happened to be located in Chicago. The staff and trustees viewed their host city as an area of interest but not as a primary focus. Not until Harold Skramstad revised the collecting scope in 1977 did CHS begin its transition from the historical society in Chicago to the Chicago Historical Society. Even as CHS staff gave more attention to Chicago-specific topics, they tended to focus on a small segment of the population. *Chicago: Creating New Traditions* and the *Chicago History Galleries* took a very narrow view of the past by celebrating the culture and traditions of only a few groups.[27] The new management structure, the renovation, and the revised mission were designed to help the staff adopt a more inclusive view, in order to transform CHS into a center for urban history research.

The biennials were an important part of this transition. In the second year of the staff enrichment program, the staff exhibition committee began planning *Prologue for a New Century,* a series of five biennial exhibitions that would examine different aspects of the city's history over the past one hundred years. Although scheduled to extend through the end of the century, the series ultimately resulted in only two exhibitions: *A City Comes of Age* and *Chicago Goes to War,* which challenged the assumption that the city's growth represented unfettered progress for everyone. Instead they argued that it was a series of negotiations between competing forces, and in doing so, they also demonstrated that race relations, poverty, and corruption were appropriate topics for museums. As with *We the People,* the biennials transformed the process by which exhibitions were conceptualized, organized, and designed.

The topics for the biennials were generated outside the institution. Prior to the establishment of the staff exhibition committee in 1987, most of the ideas for exhibitions had come from curators. The biennials disrupted this pattern. One of the goals of the biennials was to formalize CHS's partnership with academic historians. To expand the pool of available scholars, in 1988 the staff exhibition committee conducted a national search for historians who had not previously collaborated with CHS. Though CHS received only half a dozen responses, this approach signaled a more formalized process. Frustrated with the small number and poor quality of the replies, the committee decided to pair an outside historian with a staff curator. This decision was in direct response to the problems raised by using outside consultants for *We the People.* The curators and historians were only part of a larger team—each exhibition was managed by a project director and included an in-house designer and educator. For *Chicago Goes to War*, selected community members were invited to serve as advisors, and in some cases interpreters.

The biennials also encouraged the staff to expand their twentieth-century collecting efforts. For both exhibitions, the staff instituted a grassroots collecting effort that involved a public call for artifacts and for alliance building with individuals, churches, schools, and corporations that had materials from the nineteenth century. These unorthodox efforts—which eventually resulted in twenty-five hundred donations, and loans from five hundred individuals and businesses—helped demonstrate to the city's residents that their history was important. Amina Dickerson, director of education and public programs, explained that the collecting effort offered constituencies an opportunity to "see their objects and memorabilia given enhanced value in the larger context of American history and culture."[28] The planning teams not only involved residents in collecting but also invited selected members to participate in oral history projects. For *A City Comes of Age*, the exhibition team asked individuals of Lithuanian, Polish, Irish, German, and Swedish ancestry to participate in an oral history project focused on immigration and acculturation. Similarly, the *Chicago Goes to War* team turned to the African American and Japanese American communities for assistance. Because this was one of CHS's first exhibitions to document an event in remembered time, it was possible to rely upon actual informants.

The biennials' temporary status inspired the staff to experiment with the design. The Benjamin Benedict Green-Field Gallery and the A. Montgomery Ward Gallery gave the designers over six thousand square feet with which to work. It is not accurate to argue that the artifacts were subordinate to the design, but design did become, as the deputy director for research Russell Lewis explained, "a separate element that had its own presence."[29] Both of the biennials shifted from object-based exhibits to those driven by ideas; artifacts were selected for their ability to enhance learning.

The *City Comes of Age* design was based on the assumption that visitors connect to historical events when given the opportunity to examine the lives of ordinary people. The exhibition was divided into eleven major interpretive sections, which examined ethnic and racial diversity, the world of work, urban problems, public works projects, the Columbian Exposition, the vision of the city's elite, consumerism, the culture of youth, the vision of social reformers, the emergence of a civic consciousness, and the decade's legacy.[30] Instead of a linear narrative, the team created theatrical spaces that explored themes and issues. The introduction—a wall of photographs of one hundred people from the 1890s, visible from the first-floor lobby—was designed to give the impression that Chicago was the city of a million strangers. A railroad map and piled luggage introduced the concept that most people arrived in the city by rail. As visitors entered the first gallery, they were asked to pick up a small brochure that served as their ticket to the 1890s. Each slip had the picture of one of six characters, a description of his or her job, and a statement of weekly earnings. These individuals were selected because they represented diverse ethnic and economic backgrounds and spanned a wide range of experiences: George Pullman was a manufacturer and financier; Otto Link was a German woodcarver; Frank Cortello, an Italian immigrant, was a ten-year-old newspaper boy and bootblack; Mary Cassidy was an Irish maid; John Edwards was an African American day laborer; and Joseph Valewski was a thirty-year-old Polish meat trimmer in the stockyards. To reinforce the idea that it is people who make history, actors dressed as the six characters and as other historical figures important to the era, including Jane Addams, and were on hand to present dramatic monologues.

While the *City Comes of Age* designers focused on creating innovative environments, the *Chicago Goes to War* team tried to reduce every section to an intellectual concept, feeling, and color that would communicate the exhibition's overall theme that the war effort pervaded the daily lives of all Chicagoans. This strategy was based on learning objectives—an interpretive approach developed for *A House Divided* two years earlier. The learning objectives were an innovation proposed by Jim Sims, a designer from the Smithsonian's NMAH, who was hired as a consultant by the *House Divided* team. Sims proposed breaking down exhibitions into discrete sections and identifying a learning objective for each. The success of a section could be measured by what it was intended to communicate. Reducing entire sections to a single-sentence objective also helped designers, educators, and curators work together more effectively. Moving away from the book-on-the-wall model, for which *We the People* and *A House Divided* were criticized, toward a model that communicated key themes visually, the *Chicago Goes to War* team integrated learning objectives into the design by organizing the topics in concentric circles to address how the war impacted the home, the neighborhood, and the city. Prior to the opening, the staff invited a group of teachers to comment on the multitiered system. This was the first time formative evaluation was conducted by CHS with the intention of making an exhibition more user-friendly. *Chicago Goes to War* obviously benefited from the criticism that had been aimed at *We the People*. Standardizing, simplifying, and reducing the text was just one way the later team sought to make the exhibition more accessible.

The biennial teams' innovations, though, were not universally applauded. For the curatorial staff authenticity was a serious concern. The use of the six characters and artifacts of dubious provenance in *A City Comes of Age* were of special concern. All but one of the "historical" figures introduced at the beginning of the exhibition were fictional, and many of the objects used in the theatrical displays were not from the period. One purchase was particularly controversial. For the domestic environment built around Mary Cassidy, Susan Tillett had purchased a contemporary ironing board from the Kane County Flea Market. This decision stands in stark contrast to the process by which artifacts were selected for inclusion in *We the People*. Both the *City Comes of Age* and *We the People* teams had to deal with the central tension faced by museums—balancing accuracy with an appealing story. The teams simply came down on different sides of the issue.

For many of the traditionally trained curators, the *City Comes of Age* decision seemed to flout the standards of their profession. They worried that the staff had become too focused on the experience of the exhibition, at the expense of the objects. The biennial team countered by arguing that artifacts were important not because of their physical properties but because of the story they told. They should be used to illustrate rather than make arguments. In this context, history should be about lives rather than about things.

Connoisseurship, the benchmark of the curatorial profession, was no longer enough. As objects were no longer assumed to speak for themselves, the focus shifted away from the object to the label and the design. Thematic exhibitions, which relied upon a carefully argued narrative, became the norm. This raised a question as to whether CHS would be "collections driven, that is concerned primarily with the artifact and the story it represents, or mission-driven—seeking to connect the stories of the past to the reality of the present and the potential of the future in ways that more fully serve the needs of our audiences."[31] The *City Comes of Age* team agreed to be mission driven, believing that it was more important to convey an engaging message than to get everything right. While some argued that such a strategy compromised the integrity of the museum, others claimed it was possible to balance both professional standards and audience interest.

If the biennials marked a critical juncture for CHS, they also marked a critical juncture for the practitioners of urban history, which was declared a viable topic of study in 1940 by Arthur Schlesinger's essay "The City in American History." The first formal urban history association was founded in 1953.[32] By the late 1960s over fifty colleges and universities offered courses on urban history. In 1967 Charles N. Glaab's and A. Theodore Brown's *History of Urban America* was published as the field's first textbook. That same year Richard C. Wade inaugurated the "Urban Life in America" series, which ultimately resulted in twenty-four volumes. In 1970 Kenneth Jackson formed the Columbia University's Seminar on the City, and four years later the *Journal of Urban History* was founded. In the absence of a formal organization, the seminar and the *Journal* became intellectual centers of the field.[33]

Some historians were troubled by the lack of methodological cohesion and by the exclusion of the experiences of ordinary men and women. The Yale conference "The Nineteenth-Century Industrial City" in 1968 and its subsequent publication, *Nineteenth-Century Cities: Essays in the New Urban*

History edited by Stephan Thernstrom and Richard Sennett, brought these problems into bold relief. The participants/authors sought to unify and redefine the field by calling for historical inquiry into "the social dimensions of urbanization."[34] Their call for a new urban history resulted in an emphasis on urban stratification, mobility, and spatial patterns. It did not, however, unify the field. The search for an overarching conceptual framework remained elusive. In the 1980s historians reiterated the concern that the field had lost its theoretical center. Research and writing had become too focused on case studies, at the expense of discussions of larger social processes.

In response to these and other concerns, at the Organization of American Historians meeting in the spring of 1988, Kenneth Jackson suggested forming a national association. With the assistance of Richard Wade, Jackson invited urban historians to a breakfast at the American History Association meeting in December in Cincinnati to discuss the details. Fifty scholars attended what would be the first meeting of the Urban History Association (UHA). Richard Wade was elected president, and Michael Ebner was appointed executive secretary and treasurer.

Prior to the formation of the UHA, Ebner and Kathleen Conzen had established at CHS a midwestern counterpart to the Columbia seminar. In 1974 Ebner moved from the City College of New York to Lake Forest College, north of Chicago, and was frustrated to find no forum for the discussion of urban history. In 1982 he wrote to Ellsworth Brown and proposed that CHS both sponsor and become the home of a new seminar. With enthusiastic support from Brown and Russell Lewis, the Urban History Seminar was founded in 1983. It met nine times a year and helped establish an impressive network of scholars, teachers, and museum professionals interested in urban issues. Several years later, Ebner and Conzen decided that the group should host an international conference at CHS. In conjunction with their proposal, Frank Jewell of the Valentine Museum in Richmond suggested a companion conference for museum professionals, librarians, archivists, and public historians. These conferences became important catalysts to revitalize the field, and CHS's involvement helped position it as a major player in this transformation. Many of the key organizers and participants were UHA members.[35]

On October 25–27, 1990, two years after the founding of the UHA and on the fiftieth anniversary of Arthur Schlesinger's seminal essay, "The City in American History," urban historians from around the country convened at CHS to assess the state of the field. The first of the two conferences, "Modes of Inquiry for American City History," was sponsored by CHS and the *Journal of Urban History*. This was immediately followed by "Venues of Inquiry into the American City: The Place of Museums, Libraries and Archives" (October 29–30), which was sponsored by CHS, the Common Agenda project (an initiative led by the NMAH to encourage collaboration among history museums), and the Valentine Museum (a history museum in Richmond, Virginia). "Venues" addressed how to integrate current scholarship into museum practices. While some participants criticized the lack of intellectual exchange between the participants, both conferences demonstrated the need for more substantial collaborations between academics and museum professionals. "Modes" and "Venues" could not have happened at a more auspicious time for CHS. As the *City Comes of Age* biennial was on display and was the topic of a "Venues" session, it was one of the few texts under discussion that everyone had read. The conferences helped publicize the CHS biennial program and positioned CHS as a model for other history museums interested in translating cutting-edge scholarship into a forum that would be accessible to large audiences.

Although sustaining energy and enthusiasm for a decade-long exhibition program proved too difficult for CHS staff, the biennials do serve as an important interpretive benchmark. While *We the People* and *A House Divided* demonstrated that CHS staff could produce cutting-edge scholarship in a cooperative environment, the biennials transformed the process of conceptualizing, organizing, and designing exhibitions. In contrast to previous exhibitions, the ideas for the biennials were generated outside the institution. Although the biennials did not actually inaugurate team-based projects, they certainly expanded and strengthened the process. The biennials' focus on the experience of the exhibition also validated different kinds of authority. Designers, oral historians, public relations specialists, and educators were considered equal partners. More important, though, the biennials demonstrated that exhibitions and public programs at CHS no longer reflected the needs and desires of only the city's elite. Although they made an important step toward appealing to larger, more diverse audiences, the biennials did not result in an institutionwide commitment to multiculturalism, which would come instead from CHS's education department.

While Susan Tillett was brought in to coordinate the exhibition program and management of the collection, Amina Dickerson was hired in 1989 to make the institution more accessible to the public. Education witnessed more changes than any other department during this period; it grew in size and prestige and became the most visible part of the museum. The institution's increased attention to constituencies' needs can be attributed as much to Dickerson's expertise in the field as to any philosophical change on the part of the administration. As the first African American staff member in a managerial position, she became a catalyst for change. Dickerson's first goal was to hire museum educators who were philosophically committed to working with multicultural audiences. She actively recruited African American and Latino professionals, and six months after her arrival the education department was completely reorganized and restaffed.

Without a new philosophy of education, a culturally diverse staff would not by itself generate change. At most institutions, educators supply ready-made interpretations, based on the recitation of factual information, that visitors are expected to absorb passively either by going on tours or by viewing objects.[36] Such an approach assumes that visitors are empty vessels, waiting to be filled with information. In contrast, Dickerson argued that they bring a wealth of knowledge and experience to the institution, supplying another perspective from which to view institutional interpretations. Instead of telling a single story about the past, museums should offer opportunities to explore new or familiar topics in innovative ways. Doing so required that education become the expressed goal of CHS as a whole, not the responsibility of a single department. Preservation, scholarship, and interpretation all have educational functions and should involve individuals with expertise in disseminating this information to the public.

Dickerson's approach was clearly influenced by changes in the field of museum education. In the early part of the twentieth century, John Cotton Dana, Benjamin Ives Gilman, and Henry Watson Kent argued that museums should, first and foremost, be institutions dedicated to learning.[37] In the 1920s and 1930s, Arthur Melton and E. S. Robinson advocated experimental work on visitor behavior. While science centers and publicly funded museums and historical societies embraced these progressive ideas, private institutions, especially those devoted to art and history, were much less willing to democratize their operations and instead used the terms *collect, preserve,* and *interpret* to describe their primary functions. This changed in the late 1960s as the field of museum education began to take shape in the United States.

In 1969 a group of teachers and museum educators in Washington, D.C., founded the Museum Education Roundtable, and in 1973 the American Association of Museums (AAM) established its museum education committee as a standing professional committee. Chandler Screven's pioneering work on audience behavior and the formation of the AAM's committee on audience research and evaluation in 1986 legitimated audience research as a field of study. Each of these groups helped professionalize and publicize the field. In 1992 the AAM under the leadership of CHS director and AAM president Ellsworth Brown released *Excellence and Equity,* a position report of the education task force, which argued that museum audiences were as important to museums as the collections. A year earlier the AAM's code of ethics had encouraged museums to be open to the interests of different groups.[38] Dickerson, a champion of the AAM's approach, worked throughout her tenure to strengthen the links between research and interpretation, all with the aim of integrating the educational function of the institution into CHS's mission.

The process by which exhibitions were interpreted by educators was one visible manifestation of the focus on audience. CHS has always had a large cadre of dedicated volunteers responsible for giving tours and assisting with public programs. Prior to 1990, interpreter training consisted of a six-week program of lectures and workshops in which volunteers memorized key components of the exhibition and practiced sharing this information with the public. After conducting a series of exit surveys in 1990, the education staff realized that the hour-long recitation of facts—the heart and soul of the tour program—was not helping visitors learn. Confronted with an ineffective model, they began searching for another approach. Convinced that lectures were no longer a viable interpretive mechanism, they elected to use a more inquiry-based model. In this context interpreters became facilitators, and visitors were invited to disagree, discuss, debate, and most important, draw their own conclusions. Since visitors were no longer considered mere vessels to be filled, this inquiry-based approach encouraged them to become active learners. But this new model, based largely on questions and discussion, was unfamiliar to the generation of volunteers who had been trained and schooled in the more traditional manner. Several of the volunteers quit because they were afraid their authority would be undermined, but many others elected to remain and retool.

Educational programs also became more sensitive to visitors' needs. *A House Divided* was Dickerson's first major challenge. Instead of hosting traditional tours and lectures, she and the exhibition team produced a schedule of public programs designed to attract nontraditional audiences. "Voices from History," a living history program intended to bring the experiences of historical figures to life, was the most innovative addition. Because of the success of the dramatic monologues used in *A City Comes of Age,* living history interpreters dressed as Frederick Douglass, Harriet Beecher Stowe, and an enslaved woman who escaped to Canada, Susan Boggs, periodically appeared in *A House Divided* and performed for audiences. Actors portraying Abraham Lincoln and Stephen Douglas recited excerpts from their famous debates. Due to its overwhelming success, "Voices from History" became a major part of the public programming for *Chicago Goes to War, Grand Illusions,* and *Becoming American Women: Clothing and the Jewish Immigrant Experience, 1880–1920* (March 6, 1994–January 8, 1995).

While the education staff continued to organize lectures, films, school tours, and gallery talks in conjunction with specific exhibitions, they became increasingly interested in programs that extended CHS's reach. The "Sojourner Program," "Passports," and an extended collaboration with the city schools exemplify this change. The "Sojourner Program" was designed to unite professional women with young women between the ages of fourteen and twenty. During its six-month run, it served over 800 young women and involved 150 mentors. While staffing problems ultimately ended the "So-journer Program," "Passports" became more institutionalized. The education department organized an intensive two-day program focused on specific ethnic neighborhoods or enclaves—Greek, Italian, Mexican American, Jewish, Polish, African American, Korean, Chinese, Puerto Rican. Open to the public, the program began on Friday night with a dinner lecture by an urban historian or neighborhood resident and was followed by a daylong tour of a neighborhood on Saturday. By successfully linking visitors, local scholars, community leaders, and CHS staff members, "Passports" served as a bridge between the museum and local ethnic communities. Collaborations with the Chicago public schools became another way to extend the society's reach. In 1991 Cities-in-Schools, a national nonprofit organization dedicated to reducing school dropout rates among high-risk students, invited CHS to create a program for students at Lathrop Academy, Lawndale Community Academy, E. Franklin Frasier Elementary, and James Weldon Johnson Elementary School. The "History Explorers" program encouraged these West Side schools to use the museum as a primary resource through field trips and staff visits.

CHS was not the only museum in the city experimenting with innovative programs in the hope of attracting more multicultural constituencies. There were similar activities at the Art Institute of Chicago, the Field Museum of Natural History, and the Museum of Contemporary Art. Some museums went one step further to make themselves more visible at community gatherings. Beginning in 1992 the Field Museum, the Shedd Aquarium, and the Adler Planetarium set up booths at the Fiesta del Sol and the Roots International Rastafarian Give Peace a Chance Festival. Clearly CHS's activities were part of a larger trend to forge stronger museum-community linkages.

The emphasis on multiculturalism and lifelong learning required that the education staff revise the criteria they used to evaluate a particular program. For much of the society's history, a successful public program was one that drew large crowds and generated handsome revenues. But numbers, Dickerson explained, were no longer an adequate measure: "Sometimes we do great stuff, like the film programs. We show some really extraordinary films and get three people. Well sometimes those three people because of who they are . . . [are] as important as if we had seventy people who were sort of yawning and walking around." Under Dickerson's leadership, the staff educators rethought the connection between size and success and sought to define a new evaluative criteria that would measure programs by the depth, value, and meaning of the experience. A successful program fulfilled the stated learning objectives; attracted a socially, economically, culturally, and generationally diverse audience that was genuinely engaged with the speaker or performer; and generated questions, enthusiasm, requests for information, and most important, follow-up letters and telephone calls.[39] In this context, public programming had the potential to redefine the museum-constituency relationship.

Dickerson's most important legacy involved the planning of exhibitions. She was not content to accept that education was the business of a single department, and she lobbied the administration to make educators more active participants in the interpretive process. Where educators had previously inherited exhibitions, they now began to help conceptualize and plan them. Although the inclusion of educators was initially an attempt to mollify Dickerson and her staff, it eventually changed the process by which exhibitions were organized. A House Divided was the first exhibition in which educators were given equal authority over the interpretive process. This change reflected the growing understanding of learning in museums. In 1984 AAM's Museums for New Century argued that museum professionals needed to recognize that exhibitions and books communicated differently. Throughout the 1970s and 1980s, formative and summative evaluations, focus groups, and research on design encouraged museum professionals to recognize exhibitions as distinctive instruments of knowledge.[40] This body of research gave designers and educators the authority to argue that curators alone could not address the needs of the diverse constituency. The planning of A House Divided demonstrated that CHS was in step with this trend.

In the spring of 1989 the House Divided team, in an attempt to solve a design deadlock, divided the exhibition into discrete sections and identified a learning objective for each. This exercise solved two problems It unified the verbal and visual text of the exhibition and generated serious discussion about how to translate complex historical arguments into a format that would appeal to a nonacademic audience. While ostensibly intended to make the exhibition more user-friendly, the learning objectives also became a way to mediate differences between individual team members. Curators could no longer make decisions about content without input from the designers and educators, for example. The learning objectives eventually became a tangible way for educators, designers, and curators to level the playing field. As a result of the success of the learning objectives, educators became the center of the interpretive process, not just for A House Divided but for subsequent exhibitions. The institution's interpretive activities became driven by these concise statements of purpose, suggesting that visitor advocacy was becoming a new kind of authority.

All of these changes at CHS—the new management structure or staff enrichment program, the building program, the rewriting of the mission statement, the shift toward urban history, and the growing visibility of the education department—did not happen in a vacuum. During the same period, the

Valentine Museum in Richmond sponsored an ambitious staff enrichment program and began a new interpretive series focused on urban history; the Brooklyn Historical Society redefined its mission and programs; the Field Museum reorganized its entire staff into four units, going so far as to establish a department of public programs that outranked the curatorial staff in the creation of new exhibitions; the Minnesota Historical Society, Atlanta History Center, Western Pennsylvania Historical Society, and Missouri Historical Society embarked on major capital expansions; the Historical Society of Washington, D.C., and the Missouri Historical Society revised their missions; and countless other institutions revamped their education departments in order to expand their commitment to public education and lifelong learning.

Experiences at CHS, while not unique, are instructive. The changes were different ways to attend to the same question: How does an institution, which for most of its lifetime has been conservative and inward-looking, address the needs of a diverse constituency? The answer in the 1980s and 1990s was to democratize the interpretive process by embracing a new perspective on history. CHS staff's willingness to engage in this important exercise marks the distinction between innovation and change. The new mission, the 1988 addition, the biennials, and the expanded public programs were all driven by a demand for relevance. While these changes met the immediate needs of specific constituencies, they also disrupted categories of knowledge and challenged the locus of interpretive authority. Instead of viewing history as something to be imparted to an uninitiated mass, the staff began to see it as something to be explored, debated, and shared. This transition blurred the line between insiders and outsiders and changed the way decisions were made.

Moving from an object-based to an audience-based institution meant that the choices about what to collect and exhibit were no longer in the hands of curators. Participatory modes of decision making allowed designers, scholars, educators—and in the case of the biennials, constituencies—to become legitimate contributors. The CHS that emerged in the 1990s was an institution that both was aware of its obligations toward its varied constituencies and, more important, was equipped to meet them. Representing the range of historical experience was no longer the job of a single department but was, instead, the core of the institution's activities.

What is striking about this transformation is the pace and relative ease with which it was implemented. Museums are by their very nature resistant to change. Most institutions, when confronted with demands for relevance and inclusion, address the problem with what some museum scholars have called separate-but-equal programming, which often results in a multicultural exhibition being relegated to an obscure gallery. Instead of working to remedy institutional discrimination, museums have typically sought to protect the interests of their wealthy clientele.[41] That CHS did not take this path is largely because of the trustees' and the staff's vision and hard work. This is not to say that the decision was universally applauded. Several staff members who did not support the changes retired from CHS or were pressured to resign, while others viewed the changes as trendy and trivial, in part because they were imported into the institution. Had the Joyce Foundation refused to fund the *Neighborhoods: Keepers of Cultures* project in 1992, an exhibition series that continued to push interpretive boundaries, these changes might have been temporary.

CHAPTER FIVE

The *Neighborhoods* Project

[T]he interpretation of history is too important
to be left exclusively to professional historians.

—CHS, STRATEGIC PLAN, 1995

The desire to make the museum experience accessible to a wider audience is not new, but the decision to involve constituencies in the interpretive process is an innovation that has evolved as the result of several factors. The American Association of Museums, the largest and most influential organization of museum professionals in the United States, has since its founding in 1906 encouraged museums to democratize their operations. The AAM's major publications, which include *The Museum as a Social Instrument* (1942), *Museums: Their New Audience* (1972), *Museums for a New Century: A Report of the Commission on Museums for a New Century* (1984), and *Excellence and Equity: Education and the Public Dimension of Museums* (1992), have urged museums to help invest communities with a sense of ownership for their history.

The first factor is the AAM's accreditation program, founded in 1970 and designed to enhance performance and encourage self-assessment, which gives museums added incentive to engage in collaborative projects.[1] The only formal standardized measure of quality in the museum field, this accreditation measures an institution's governance and technical processes. It evaluates the depth of the institution's commitment to its audiences and has directly influenced other professional museum organizations, notably the American Association for State and Local History.

The second factor to shift the balance of power in museums came from Native American activists who had tried for decades to gain control over the collection and display of the artifacts and remains of their ancestors. In support of their efforts, Congress passed the American Indian Religious Freedom Act on August 11, 1978. This was the first legislation to encourage museums and other research institutions to cooperate with native communities when studying and displaying their history. Although the AIRFA encouraged a new level of sensitivity, it did not resolve the problem of repatriation. Native groups continued to lobby for control over sacred objects and ultimately helped pass the Native American Graves Protection and Repatriation Act (NAGPRA) on November 16, 1990, which permanently altered the relationship between museums and their collections and constituencies. In concert with AAM's initiatives to make museums more accessible, NAGPRA inaugurated the era of cooperation between museums and communities that eventually spread to include other previously marginalized groups. Although NAGPRA applies to a relatively small category of objects and most directly affects natural history museums, professionals in history and art museums immediately recognized the importance of such partnerships.

The third factor is the transfer of authority from institutions to individuals. In *The Authority of Experts,* Thomas Haskell traces the erosion of authority in law and medicine to the skeptical mood of the 1970s. The medical malpractice crisis, led in 1977 by plaintiffs in New York and California and exacerbated by soaring medical costs, threatened the autonomy of physicians. Additionally, the Federal Trade Commission's challenge to the American Medical Association's standards of accreditation, which undermined their near exclusive control over the profession reflected the tide of changing opinion. Lawyers were not immune from the same level of public scrutiny. The *Goldfarb* decision in 1975, which exposed the anticompetitive practices of local bar associations, held that lawyers were not exempt from the Sherman Anti-Trust Act. As a result, the federal government filed a series of anticompetitive suits against engineers, architects, and other learned, professional groups. Haskell argues that these seemingly unrelated examples suggest that a university-trained elite should not be trusted with complete authority. The curriculum and canon struggles documented by the academic and popular press and embodied by the debates over the national history standards (see the Introduction) indicate that the distrust that spread to college campuses in the 1980s and 1990s was part of this trend.[2]

Beleaguered by controversies over exhibitions, museums are having to answer the question: What is the nature of expert authority? The answer indicates that the role of the curator, like that of the doctor, lawyer, or university professor, has changed radically.[3] Once revered as unquestioned authorities in their fields, curators have seen their rights to interpret the past challenged by new experts—who might just as likely be ordinary people who have experienced history as people who have studied it. Collaborative and community-based projects are an outgrowth of this sea change.

Museums embarked on collaborative projects more in order to survive than because of any shift in philosophy. The fourth factor is demographic change in urban areas over the past half century. As the white middle class moved to the suburbs, inner cities became populated by new immigrants and dispossessed agricultural and unskilled workers. As in most major cities, the percentage of residents in Chicago who do not speak English as their first language has been on a steady rise since the 1960s. These trends have isolated many museums from their traditional audience. Concurrent with these demographic shifts, traditional bases of support have steadily eroded. With a dwindling list of multimillion-dollar donors, museums have recognized that they must tap into new audiences in order to survive in an increasingly competitive marketplace. Realizing that these new audiences have different needs, interests, and demands, museum professionals have begun addressing issues that are relevant to their local constituencies, providing more extensive outreach programs, and most important, asking for community input in programs and exhibitions.

The crisis in public education also encouraged museums to engage in collaborative projects. Two reports published in the early 1980s, *A Nation at Risk* and *Educating Americans for the 21st Century,* chronicled the problems plaguing the nation's schools (such as high dropout rates, poor performance on tests, widespread violence, and lack of preparedness for teachers and students) and called for radical reforms. Both recommended that schools work with museums and other institutions of informal learning. Eager to extend their reach into the community, museums around the country established formal programs with school districts and found that such initiatives were attractive to funders. In 1987 CHS president Ellsworth Brown explained: "We could have 'sold' our education department three times last year to eager corporations while pleading for general operational support."[4]

The National Endowment for the Humanities and the National Endowment for the Arts have also played an important role in promoting collaborative ventures. Established in 1965, both the NEH and the NEA provide funding with the intention of improving the American public's access to the arts and humanities. They have led the way in requiring, as a condition of their support, that museums utilize academic scholars—and more recently, community residents—to engage in collaborative projects. In addition to outright grants the NEA and NEH distribute matching and challenge grants, which insist that recipients secure funds from private sources.[5] This model has influenced the activities of foundations and corporations, who, lacking access to academic peer review networks, use national support to measure the quality of a particular program. Institutions that rely on federal funds must meet certain guidelines, the most important of which is accessibility. These guidelines have encouraged corporations and foundations to follow suit.

All of these factors encouraged and, in some cases required, cultural institutions to share authority with their local constituencies. One of the earliest strategies involved establishing neighborhood, branch, or satellite museums. Inspired by the possibilities and tired of waiting for other institutions to follow the Smithsonian's example, local communities began forming their own museums. Ethnic museums tend to be firmly rooted in community life and involve local residents in partnerships at a much higher degree than mainstream museums. The Anacostia Museum in Washington, D.C. (1967), the Studio Museum of Harlem (1968), the DuSable Museum in Chicago (1968), the Japanese American National Museum in Los Angeles (1985), and the Chinatown History Museum in New York City (1990) are visible and successful examples. Each of these museums sent a powerful message to mainstream institutions: share authority or lose your audience.

In response to internal and external pressures, mainstream museums began a period of self-examination in the 1970s, and many elected to reallocate their resources in order to begin serving the broader community. The Oakland Museum reopened expanded galleries in 1969 and began hosting programs focused on the African American, Asian American, and Native American residents in the Bay Area. In 1971 the Metropolitan Museum of Art formed a department of community programs, the Museum of the City of New York initiated a series of community projects, and the American Museum of Natural History developed an education program to attract African American and Caribbean constituencies. Other museums followed the same path and widened their outreach, but few of these programs were designed to be truly collaborative, and even fewer resulted in significant institutional change.[6]

When it became clear that they could not gain widespread community support through traditional outreach programs, several institutions proposed projects that would give previously marginalized communities a sense of ownership of their history, and in turn, of the museum. Especially popular in large urban institutions, collaborative projects have provided an impetus to question who owns history. The Brooklyn Historical Society, the Brooklyn Children's Museum, the Missouri Historical Society, and the Minnesota Historical Society have used collaborations to formalize institutional change. Throughout the 1980s and 1990s, these and other institutions throughout the country organized advisory committees, held community meetings, implemented outreach programs, and invited residents to participate in the interpretive process. Although the individual initiatives varied one from another, all the participating museums struggled to share authority at an institutional level. CHS embarked on one of the nation's most ambitious programs, *Neighborhoods: Keepers of Culture*, and this presents an opportunity to examine the issues and problems raised by collaborative exhibitions, for the purpose of determining what role museums can realistically be expected to play in civic life. The first two exhibitions in the four-part series had the greatest impact on the way CHS sought to reconstitute interpretive authority.

Neighborhoods was not the first project that required CHS staff to work with community partners outside their traditional membership pool, but it was the first that was explicitly designed to formalize these relationships. On May 28, 1992, the Joyce Foundation issued a call for proposals for collaborative projects between cultural institutions and local communities that would deal "directly with issues of pluralism" and that would make "Chicago's rich array of cultural resources more widely accessible to traditional and non-traditional audiences." The goal was to help mainstream cultural organizations become "more responsive to the urban community."[7] In December 1992 the foundation awarded $100,000 to CHS (less than a third of the $310,000 that was requested); a second pledge of $75,000 was made in April 1995.

The experimental nature of the project resulted in what CHS president Douglas Greenberg refers to as a series of "miscalculations" by CHS. *Neighborhoods* started out as a documentation project with a small exhibition component. Early in the planning phase of *Douglas/Grand Boulevard: The Past and the Promise,* however, the decision was made to change the project to a major exhibition series, which posed budget and staffing problems that the exhibition teams never really overcame. CHS fully expected the Joyce Foundation pledge to cover the majority of the costs, but in the end the size and scope of the project eventually meant that the pledge would provide only part of the support.

To select the actual neighborhoods CHS recruited community activists and also academics who specialized in urban or neighborhood history to serve on an advisory committee. The committee members agreed that they should focus on how specific ethnic groups interact within a given geographical region, but they found it more problematic to limit the project to four neighborhoods, which were then meant to be representative of the city's population. Originally presented with a list of thirty neighborhoods, the committee was to select areas that were geographically, ethnically, historically, and economically diverse. The committee elected to pair contiguous neighborhoods, and the final selections Douglas/Grand Boulevard, Rogers Park/West Ridge, Pilsen/Little Village, and Near West Side/East Garfield Park allowed for a more representative offering.[8] After the neighborhoods were selected, the advisory committee continued to meet periodically, but the responsibility for organizing each neighborhood exhibition then shifted to CHS staff.

With the promise of $100,000 from the Joyce Foundation and with an application for $175,000 pending with the Robert R. McCormick Tribune Foundation, Douglas Greenberg, the director of three months, committed CHS to raise the money for all four exhibitions. This was no small decision. Over 75 percent of the CHS budget was reserved for fixed costs, which left very little money for exhibitions and public programs. The decision to move forward with *Neighborhoods*—as with *We the People* a decade earlier—

suggested that it was an institutional priority. The most tangible manifestation of the society's commitment was the search for a project coordinator.

In December 1993 director of curatorial affairs Russell Lewis hired Tracye
Matthews, a twenty-seven-year-old doctoral candidate in American history
from the University of Michigan. A native of the Midwest, Matthews was active in community and campus politics in Detroit and Ann Arbor and had
experience with grassroots organizing. Her presence was important for several reasons. The project had been unfocused for over a year; Matthews's arrival gave it the legitimacy and visibility it needed within CHS. Additionally,
as an African American woman, she was able to help CHS build trust within
nonwhite communities. Although not from Chicago, Matthews's race gave
her the status of an insider that a white coordinator would not have enjoyed.
Her leadership skills and academic credentials reassured the residents that
their history would be fairly and accurately represented.

Sharing authority became an important part of *Neighborhoods,* and inter-
nally this meant involving the noncuratorial staff in interpretive decisions.[9]
Although logistical issues eventually made it impractical, this goal was reflected in the composition of the early teams. Each core team was composed of
four or five CHS staff members who had a particular set of skills that was
deemed important. The staff was not given any input into how the teams were
organized and in most cases were assigned to neighborhoods about which they
knew very little. The desire to share interpretive authority posed some serious
problems at the outset. One curator noted that "it is a noble idea but I can't go
into the accounting office and tend to the books so why are we expecting an
accountant to come over here and curate an exhibition?"[10]

To help this disparate group function effectively, Matthews in her first two
months on the job turned to outside consultants for assistance. Dennis Jen-
nings and Robert Shropshire of the Institute of Cultural Affairs conducted a
team-building workshop for fourteen staff members involved in the *Neighborhoods* project. Because some of the members had not previously worked on
exhibitions or in teams, they needed to learn how to facilitate meetings,
work cooperatively, and become responsive to the residents' needs. This
same group participated in three daylong consensus-building and diversity-
awareness workshops. Not satisfied that this experience adequately prepared
them for the task at hand, Matthews encouraged the teams to familiarize
themselves with the relevant scholarship. In April 1994 she hired Susan
O'Halloran from Clergy and Laity Concerned (CALC) and the Racism Reduction Institute to conduct two four-hour antiracism workshops. To keep the
staff thinking and talking about these issues, Matthews also organized an in-
house brown-bag lunch series from August to November 1994, where staff
members could discuss prejudice, racism, tolerance, and stereotyping. As a
result, the *Neighborhoods* teams were becoming pockets of progressiveness.

In spite of some minor adjustments, the planning process for each exhibition was divided into six stages: preplanning, recruitment, exhibition planning, opening, public programming, and relocation. During preplanning, the in-house team worked to familiarize itself with the local history. This was an informal process in *Douglas/Grand Boulevard,* and also in *Rogers Park* until its curator, Scott La France, withdrew from the project. Because the team had not been working as a group, for several months it had to scramble to catch up. Learning from the *Rogers Park* experience, the *Pilsen* team members relied on traditional and nontraditional sources to familiarize themselves with the neighborhood's history; they incorporated readings into their weekly meetings and invited Louise Kerr, Dominic Pacyga, and Maria Benfield to lecture at several lunch meetings. In addition, this team videotaped seven dialogues with community members. At these informal meetings, longtime residents of Pilsen and Little Village were invited to discuss themes and topics that ranged from Czech sokols (sports and health organizations established in the mid-nineteenth century) to the Gads Hill settlement (a Presbyterian settlement house focused on serving working-class immigrants).

Recruitment required a keen sensitivity to the individual neighborhood's social and political landscape. As an African American woman, Matthews assumed correctly that the residents of Douglas/Grand Boulevard would respond to CHS's request for assistance if she were to coordinate the first stages of outreach. In Rogers Park the most active organizations tended to serve white middle-class constituencies, and for this reason Scott La France (both white and middle-class) directed most of the outreach in this neighborhood. This division of labor should not give the impression that other members of the teams were not involved. Longtime CHS employees Olivia Mahoney and Archie Motley had already established contacts with Douglas/Grand Boulevard residents, and they helped Matthews target organizations, compile lists, and make phone calls. The teams achieved varied rates of success. By soliciting the assistance of Sokoni Karanja, Timuel Black, and Leroy Kennedy—three community gatekeepers—the *Douglas/Grand Boulevard* group was able to tap into a network of community organizations that had a long history of grassroots organizing, including the Mid-South Planning and Development Commission, the Center for New Horizons, the Elliott Donnelley Youth Center, and Partners in Community Development. In contrast, the *Rogers Park* team was unable to gain access to members of the Caribbean, Orthodox Jewish, and East Indian communities because they were unable to recruit the necessary community partners. As a result many of the newer *Rogers Park* immigrants were not active participants in the CHS interpretation of their history.

The planning phase for each exhibition, from the first community meeting to the public opening, averaged ten months. Although CHS did not formally outline the community partners' roles, they were expected to participate at every level of the exhibition process. This meant suggesting themes for the exhibition, identifying additional participants and informants, reading label copy, locating artifacts, serving on committees, participating in oral history projects, advertising locally, and developing public programs. As liaisons between CHS and the local community, the partners helped the society staff negotiate local cultural dynamics. By including outsiders in a process normally reserved for and restricted to insiders, CHS sought to transform exhibit making into a form of public discourse.[11] Although CHS had used community members as advisors for previous exhibitions, *Neighborhoods* sought to fundamentally alter the balance of power. Evaluating its success requires a careful analysis of the issues and problems raised during the process.

Participation in the monthly meetings for *Douglas/Grand Boulevard* and *Rogers Park* was inconsistent, and it soon became clear to CHS staff that by its very nature the process was exclusive. Although each team worked to diversify the participants in terms of age, race, ethnicity, and economic background, the community partners were a self-selecting group. The individuals who did not participate were often suspicious of white institutions coming in to do their history. For many new immigrants to Chicago, mainstream museums represented the repressive governments they were trying to escape. For *Neighborhoods*, the lack of participation was primarily a question of logistics. Many residents held night jobs, making evening meetings inconvenient. Even though CHS insisted on holding the meetings in the community, few residents could make a regular commitment. This was especially a problem, Matthews argues, for recent immigrants. To complicate matters, the project was based on the assumption that a neighborhood was a geographic and social space that linked individuals through a shared set of experiences. But this was an artificial construct for some, who did not recognize their physical surroundings and geographic proximity as being more important than family, work, church, or ethnic affiliation. For this reason, they did not have any compelling reason to participate.

Comfort was another issue. At the follow-up meeting for *Rogers Park* in Warren Park, one community partner explained that certain members of the Latino community were reluctant to participate because they felt themselves silenced by more vocal members of the group who professed a certain ideology.[12] Language barriers also formed part of the problem. CHS staff offered to have translators at meetings and to make the exhibitions available to non–English-speaking audiences, but this did not happen until *Pilsen*. This is not to say that the individual teams did not make other efforts. Throughout the planning process, each team experimented with ways to build trust and to forge new relationships. They sponsored oral history training, conservation workshops, and a mural project with the hope that they would widen the net. Despite these efforts, CHS never gained the kind of representation it had anticipated.

The desire to involve the community's diverse populations in the exhibition process became a real problem for the *Rogers Park* team. According to the 1990 U.S. census, Rogers Park is one of the nation's most culturally diverse neighborhoods. Between 1980 and 1990 the white population decreased from 77 percent to under 50 percent, the African American population tripled, and Hispanic, Asian, and other nonwhite groups grew in numbers.[13] The different populations remained segregated from each other. Longtime white residents were very active in the planning stages, but CHS staff struggled to gain access to the Jamaican, Belizian, Haitian, Mexican, and Orthodox Jewish communities. Driven by the desire to represent everybody, they delayed making major decisions, which ultimately threatened the project's success.

Despite the problems generated by this strategy, their instincts were correct. The most vocal participants in *Rogers Park* were eager to celebrate the neighborhood's diversity but never gave much thought to what this actually meant. The team's inability to address these issues in a critical fashion resulted in an exhibition that failed to explain historical trends, which became a problem for visitors, some of whom complained that the exhibition was incoherent, simplistic, and patronizing:

There are no opinions offered, no angles presented. What is there to agree or disagree with?

The exhibition is too much of a jumble, and the sense of continuity is lost.

There is too little coordination of objects and *no* consideration to chronological exposition.

I'd like to see more analysis of why things change over time, rather than just how.

The blind adherence to current jargon and deforming of history in terms of the fashionable tilt toward multiculturalism as both object and subject destroys the potential historical and educational value of your exhibition.[14]

These responses indicate that the planning team at some level had underestimated the visitors' needs. Expecting a coherent narrative, visitors also wanted a context in which to understand change over time, something *Rogers Park* did not deliver.

The experimental nature of the project meant that the exhibition teams did not have a clear sense of what collaboration entailed. It quickly became clear that success, at least for CHS, depended on the degree of cooperation with the neighborhood residents. Not all of the community partners agreed.

Compare two answers to the question "How would you evaluate the collaboration?" The first response is from a *Douglas/Grand Boulevard* partner, the second from a *Rogers Park* partner:

The staff worked very hard. They were fortunate enough and thoughtful enough to reach and get volunteers . . . and one of the positive things [is] that we began to operate like a team. A family kind of arrangement, the give and take within the meetings was constructive and friendly. If there was criticism it was not derisive. That's one of the outcomes that one did not think about. Which evolved, which helped it to make the exhibit itself more enjoyable for all those.

It is important to keep in mind that this is community work. I do a lot of community work, and very rarely is it comfortable and to a great extent it's easy to say a lot of the discomfort is racial, ethnic, based on class, but every community project I do is uncomfortable. It's just an uncomfortable process whatever your color, class, or ethnicity. It's uncomfortable for rich white people to come to these meetings. That's something that people have to remember as well. It's uncomfortable for everybody to come and sit with a bunch of strangers.[15]

Discussions about the exhibition script revealed the differences between the two groups. CHS staff working on *Douglas/Grand Boulevard* assumed that the community partners wanted to be involved in writing the label copy. In fact, the partners were willing to comment on drafts, but they expected the staff to use their skills and expertise in constructing the narrative. The larger group was not so naïve as to assume that CHS would give up its total authority and, as Tracye Matthews put it, "genuflect to the people."[16] Instead of trying to have the entire group work on every facet of the project, the *Douglas/Grand Boulevard* team divided into committees composed of CHS staff and community members who were responsible for reporting back to the larger group. While *Rogers Park* relied upon a similar committee structure, the community partners were more concerned about monitoring what story would be told and wanted to review all of the written text.

The *Douglas/Grand Boulevard* team agreed on the exhibition's format and themes early in the process. On the other hand, the *Rogers Park* team struggled over what counted as history, and the debate over how much space to devote to contemporary issues—referred to by some community partners as sociology—raised a much more troubling problem. For many of the older partners, urban renewal, the influx of Asian, Caribbean, and African American residents, and the problems with gangs and drugs occurred after 1945 and thus did not belong in a history exhibition. The objection to a sociological approach masked the fact that *multiculturalism* as a word was used often but without much precision. There was little open discussion of racism within the neighborhood or at the community meetings; instead, references to race became encoded, unspoken, and invisible. Class and racial tensions were embedded in discussions over what story should be told. Several community partners wanted to focus on how the neighborhood "used to be" before "those people moved in."[17] Individuals who referred to streets as crowded, filthy, and dangerous were also the ones pushing the team to exhibit the distant past.

The entire *Neighborhoods* project was criticized both inside and outside the institution for avoiding difficult topics. There are several factors that mitigated against a more critical approach. The most active participants tended to be community elders who had a personal stake in avoiding controversial issues. The status of the CHS staff as outsiders and the inexperience of the youth videographers (teenagers conducted and videotaped interviews) made it difficult for both groups to probe or challenge residents' understanding of the past. For these reasons the label copy and the video interviews emphasized survival and success in the face of overwhelming odds. CHS staff had to constantly battle against nostalgia. While the *Douglas/Grand Boulevard* partners discussed the 1919 race riot, restrictive covenants, and other overt forms of prejudice, they were reluctant to talk about the departure of many middle-class African Americans for better housing elsewhere. The team could not arrive at a compromise over how to include information about gangs, teen pregnancy, and violence—so these topics were omitted from the script.

Contemporary issues were not the only taboos. Some residents of Douglas/Grand Boulevard made their money playing the numbers or running illegal jitneys [cabs] and prostitution rings, but these topics were noticeably absent from the exhibition script.[18] The passage of time did little to make these topics more palatable. *Douglas/Grand Boulevard* curator Olivia Mahoney explained: "for the first go around of their history . . . I just didn't feel like we could get too in-depth."[19] Similarly, the *Rogers Park* partners did not want to stress any of the negatives. With the exception of a small section on CAPS (the Chicago Alternative Policing Strategy, a partnership of police, community, and city agencies founded in 1993 in five of Chicago's police districts), the problem of gangs, drugs, crime, and violence were not mentioned in the exhibition.

This avoidance of controversial topics did not escape the notice of several survey respondents who criticized CHS for its myopic, romanticized view of the neighborhood. One wrote in response to a question asking what visitors would like to see changed, omitted, or added: "Rogers Park is a very high crime area. It should have been noted. Especially the increase in gangs/drugs." Another wrote: "Exhibit seems to accentuate the positive and glosses over some of the problems faced by the community. It almost seems like you see it through rose-colored glasses."[20] The *Pilsen* team took a somewhat different approach and elected to probe issues of racism, poverty, and violence. But its honesty had limitations. The struggle it foregrounded was limited to intergroup relations at the expense of investigations of intragroup tensions. The subtitles of the first two exhibitions betray an emphasis on the positive: *Douglas/Grand Boulevard: The Past and the Promise* and *Rogers Park/West Ridge: Rhythms of Diversity.* The final two exhibitions, *Pilsen/Little Village: Our Home, Our Struggle* and *Rooting, Uprooting: The West Side,* suggest those teams' willingness to address difficult topics.

The tendency to minimize conflict is part of a larger pattern. The recovery of the history of marginalized groups must pass through three distinct phases. The first phase is focused on identifying notable individuals; the second analyzes their contributions; then, only when historians have passed through these two stages can they begin to address the complexity and diversity of experience.[21] Each phase is a necessary step toward presenting a more complete historical narrative. This pattern is familiar to academic historians, but it is more problematic for museum professionals. Most museums have failed to reach the third phase, because they tend to skirt around controversy and conflict, ostensibly to cater to the delicate sensibilities of their constituencies. It may be true that people come to CHS to be entertained, not to contemplate the problem of prostitution in South Chicago, but it may also be true that they might find such a difficult topic worth exploring.[22]

How, then, can museums engaged in collaborative projects balance accuracy with advocacy? At CHS the process that was undertaken to organize each exhibition was a struggle to negotiate opposite ends of this spectrum. During the preplanning and recruitment phases, the staff worked to become trusted outreach workers, but in the actual planning they were expected to be critical historians.[23] The project seemed to have two incompatible goals: first to analyze and then to celebrate the history of the neighborhood. Achieving the first goal offended some of the community partners; achieving the second required omitting evidence, overlooking conflict, and most troubling, erasing significant players from the historical record.

Neighborhoods was intended to be inclusive, but to empower some groups meant disempowering others. Determining who had the authority to tell their stories was as political a process as that of selecting the neighborhoods. Although *Douglas/Grand Boulevard* did not become the center of African American business and cultural life in Chicago until 1920, 80 percent of the exhibition was focused on the history of this one population. Irish Catholics, white Protestants, and German Jews, groups that the curator Olivia Mahoney called silent partners, founded institutions that had been—and in some cases still are—integral parts of the neighborhood's economic, social, and political life. Unfortunately, their history was not politically correct enough to be placed front and center. Mahoney explains why: "It [was] really time to do African American history."[24] Even though she continually pushed the team to compare migratory patterns and contemporary issues, the connections were only tenuously made. This became more noticeable when *Douglas/Grand Boulevard* moved to the DuSable Museum, where the curator Ramon Price removed the biographies of whites and edited the first section so that it discussed only Native American settlement, essentially erasing early residents from the historical record.

The *Rogers Park* planning team faced a similar problem. In their attempt to appeal to the current residents, team members overlooked an important part of the neighborhood's past. In an editorial to the *Chicago Tribune,* Theodore Berland, the past president of the North Town Community Council, criticized the exhibition for failing to include "the Scandinavians who settled in the area in the last century, the Irish and German Catholics who built homes and churches . . . in the early 20th Century and the Jews who completed the building of the community with their homes, synagogues and community centers in the middle of the century."[25]

While some visitors, CHS staff members, and community partners criticized *Neighborhoods* for being too laudatory, several local museum professionals argued that it trespassed on their turf. Margaret Burroughs, the founder of the DuSable Museum, worried that the *Neighborhoods* project duplicated the mission, purpose, and programming of the DuSable and thus might threaten to put them out of business: "I fear that when this project goes public it will be interpreted by the African-American community as an instrument to undermine the DuSable Museum, consciously or not." Her comments exposed the tenuous funding situation that plagues community-based museums, and her charge of cultural trespassing was not without grounds. Carlos Tortolero, executive director of the Mexican Fine Arts Center Museum and a community partner for *Pilsen,* argued that traditionally Eurocentric museums are rewarded for embracing multiculturalism before demonstrating the depth of their commitment.[26] While CHS had been working in partnership with the DuSable staff for much of the planning phase of *Douglas/Grand Boulevard,* they had not seriously considered Burroughs's suggestion of sharing the exhibition and public programs. Out of this incident came the idea to move the exhibitions into the communities themselves.

In spite of the conflicts and debates spiraling around the project, the planning teams remained focused on attracting diverse audiences to the individual exhibitions. They hoped to appeal to nonresidents, but their greatest concern was with the young people from their own communities. The planning teams came up with three options: youth-produced videos, hands-on interactive components, and neighborhood postcards. The videos involved teenagers in the planning process, the interactives appealed to children, and the postcards provided residents with an opportunity to record and display memories of their neighborhood. All three features required different kinds of expertise.

Early in the planning of *Douglas/Grand Boulevard,* Matthews invited Tony Streit, a local videographer experienced in working with high-risk teenagers, to help coordinate a series of youth-produced videos for each neighborhood. His companies, Street-Level Video and Live Wire Youth Media Video, were established to give urban youths access to new media technology. For each neighborhood Streit recruited about a dozen teenage residents to conduct and edit interviews. The process of editing the tapes allowed the youths to discover that the process of writing history was not just about ordering the facts. As they watched other documentaries and conducted their own ethnographic research, Streit urged them to consider the editorial decisions that must be made in order to give the impression of either consensus or conflict. In doing so he helped them understand the role they played as mediators between informants and museum visitors. As artifacts, the videos offered visitors the same lesson. Instead of presenting a single story of a particular neighborhood, they offered complementary, occasionally competing, versions. Seeing the residents speak for themselves, visitors came away with a sense that history is a series of stories about the past.

While the videos involved teenagers, the interactives were designed to appeal to children, an audience CHS had been trying to attract. Largely responsible for the inclusion of this new component, the staff educators encouraged the *Neighborhoods* teams to develop gallery activities for those visitors who were too young to read the label copy or too short to view the artifacts. The first three exhibitions included interactives. *Douglas/Grand Boulevard* featured several games such as "Create a Neighborhood," "Plan a Weekend in Bronzeville, 1935–45" (Bronzeville is the name given to the area in the 1920s when it became the center of black business and cultural life), and the "Housing Game." The *Rogers Park* team elected to expand the activities; the "Annexation Puzzle" and "Find Me Rings" were clearly geared toward children aged from four to eleven, while the "Mystery Mailboxes" and "Jukebox" had a wider appeal. The *Pilsen* team created Czech, Mexican, and Polish versions of hopscotch, and the "Village Diner" allowed visitors to create a breakfast using food props representing Native American, Czech, and Mexican cuisines.

Although adults tend to be as captivated by videos and interactives as children, the resource centers were specifically designed for adult use. For each exhibition, the designers arranged tables and chairs for rest and reflection. Newspapers, bulletins, and periodicals relating to the neighborhood were available for review. Additionally, CHS provided postcards for former residents to record their memories of the neighborhood. Once the postcard was completed, the former resident had the option to post it for other visitors to read. For visitors to record more general reactions to the exhibition, the staff placed a notebook at the exit. Responses varied from single sentence praises ("As a Rogers Park citizen I want to thank everyone for giving me a new outlook on my neighborhood") to nuanced critiques ("In contrast to the last neighborhood exhibit and other museum exhibits here, the Rogers Park exhibit is practically correct, but incoherent, lacking historical trends and real educational value").[27] Each week the cards and the responses from the notebook were gathered and distributed to key members of the *Neighborhoods* teams.

While CHS had been promoting *Neighborhoods* as a major exhibition, the opening for *Douglas/Grand Boulevard* indicated the initial limits of the institution's support. As the date grew near, the membership office informed Tracye Matthews and Russell Lewis that the community would not be invited to the opening, because CHS exhibition openings are restricted to museum members who pay for the privilege to attend. Geared toward donors and local dignitaries, they are catered, black-tie affairs that are still reported in the social pages of the *Chicago Tribune*. Such an event seemed at odds with the *Neighborhoods* goals to attract previously underserved audiences. Although initially a logistical nightmare, the lack of support from membership actually freed the *Douglas/Grand Boulevard* team to host a more democratic gathering. The team raised additional money, and Matthews and Lewis took over the responsibility for making the necessary arrangements. Advertising it, though, would prove more difficult. Prior to the opening the public relations manager, Pat Kremer, left CHS to join the staff at the Field Museum. To compensate, Lewis and Matthews worked through the exhibition's public relations and outreach committee to advertise locally. Timuel Black encouraged local ministers to announce the opening to their congregations, Matthews spoke on local public and ethnic radio stations, and she and Black appeared together on a local cable show.[28] Their efforts were rewarded when over nine hundred people attended the opening. The DuSable high school band played; Douglas Greenberg, Matthews, and Black spoke; and a local technical school donated a six-foot cake depicting a street scene in Bronzeville. Members of the planning team helped serve food and worked as ushers and security guards to help cut costs. To ensure that residents would have adequate transportation, CHS hired school buses to shuttle between the neighborhood and the society. The success of the *Douglas/Grand Boulevard* opening helped encourage the administration to underwrite the openings for the other three exhibitions.

Although well-attended, the openings brought into bold relief some problems that had long plagued the planning teams. Each exhibition was originally meant to be organized in less than a year. What would probably have been a tight schedule for any conventional exhibition became a major problem for *Neighborhoods*. The staff clearly felt the stress, as did the community partners. Some interpreted the time frame as a lack of commitment on the part of the host institution. One community partner argued that the cursory attention to the most difficult topics was the direct result of the deadlines imposed by CHS.[29] The placement of the exhibition in the Colonel Robert R. McCormick South Atrium Gallery was also a problem. Instead of a formal gallery, the exhibitions were located in what appears to be a walkway or lobby. Traffic patterns encouraged visitors to walk past the installation. Aware of this problem, the *Pilsen* team erected a wall near the entrance and moved the resource center and hopscotch games to the front of the gallery to attract visitors. Unlike the American history wing, where the galleries are built to fit the existing space, the *Neighborhoods* projects felt temporary. *West Side,* the final exhibition, moved to the Greenfield Gallery and was thus provided with a more formal exhibition space.

Time and space concerns exacerbated staffing and budget problems. Matthews was the only staff member hired to work on *Neighborhoods,* and the rest of the participants had to volunteer their time. To complicate matters the CHS fund-raising efforts came under scrutiny. From the perspective of the administration, the $575,000 raised for the four exhibitions was adequate in light of the circumstances. This position, though, was not widely shared by the staff or community partners. The *Neighborhoods* budget was often compared to the budget for *The Last Best Hope of Earth: Abraham Lincoln and the Promise of America* (February 12, 1996–February 13, 1997), a traveling exhibition not curated by CHS and for which the development office raised $500,000. Staff members argued that if the *Neighborhoods* project was an institutional priority, then staff and resources should be marshaled to support it. The staff working on *Neighborhoods* were frequently asked by the community partners to explain why such a rich institution as CHS would underfund the project. In retrospect Greenberg offered a possible explanation for their discontent: "I don't think we ever showed people what was involved on the money side. And I know we never explained about the issue of fixed costs, which actually drives so much of what we do."[30] Greenberg's response highlights the problem that many museums face: budgets that cover operating costs, salaries, and other major expenses are approved a year in advance and do not allow for additional exhibitions, such as *Neighborhoods,* that cost thousands of dollars.

Assigning credit and recognition became another problem. In their attempt to realize the goals of the project, the organizers of the openings downplayed the contributions of some of the key players. This was a particular problem for *Douglas/Grand Boulevard.* Olivia Mahoney, for example, has had a long and illustrious career at CHS. She is one of the institution's most experienced and creative curators. She is also white. Although she curated *Douglas/Grand Boulevard,* at the opening she was not invited to speak, in violation of an unwritten custom in the museum world. CHS's adoption of a policy in 1987 to attribute creative and scholarly work on exhibitions made Mahoney's absence more striking, however.[31] Realizing it was not politically savvy to credit a white authority figure, Mahoney consented to stay in the background. Ironically, while the community members were foregrounded at the opening, they did not receive the same billing in the press releases, which listed exhibit developers, exhibit content specialists, and designers but made no mention of the community partners.

Unlike other collaborative projects at CHS, the opening did not signal the end of the community partnership. Because of their desire to promote the exhibition, many of the partners remained active in the public programming. They worked with local teachers to prepare curriculum packets, helped organize workshops, trained interpreters, and in some cases became interpreters. The *Douglas/Grand Boulevard* and *Pilsen* partners advertised programs that would help revitalize the community, and they developed intergenerational dialogues, arts and crafts workshops, and lectures. The *Rogers Park* and *West Side* teams were more interested in celebratory events, which included walking tours, arts fairs, seminars, and film festivals. Most of the activity, though, was focused on moving the exhibition into the community. One of *Neighborhoods* goals was to produce a tangible product that could be given to the residents, but moving the exhibition from CHS to the neighborhood raised a new set of issues.

The DuSable Museum, the host for *Douglas/Grand Boulevard,* made substantial interpretive changes. Although these alterations were ostensibly made so as to fit the exhibition to the space, they essentially reduced the exhibition to a celebration of Bronzeville. After its run at the DuSable, the exhibition was slated to be moved to the Supreme Life Building, but Harold Lucas, one of the community partners, was unable to secure the space. For *Rogers Park,* the community partners and CHS could not find a willing host; the most promising possibility, Loyola University, did not have available space. Ultimately, elements of the exhibition components were given to the Rogers Park/West Ridge Historical Society. *West Side* was slated for display at the Duncan YMCA, but the arrangements fell through. The most successful relocation came with *Pilsen's* move to the Mexican Fine Arts Center Museum in June 1997. All of the exhibitions have now been dismantled, the loan items have been returned to the lenders, and except for the materials associated with *Rogers Park* the exhibition components are stored at CHS.

Although not intentional, the four-part exhibition's move out of CHS signaled the formal end of the collaboration. The *Neighborhoods* project was built upon the experience of the planning of the exhibition and subsequent programs. When the activity that sustained the relationship ended, so did much of the relationship. Many residents found themselves with a lot of enthusiasm for community history, but with very little sense of what to do next. When the monthly meetings ended, the partners lost regular access to the staff. Many CHS staff members remained in close contact with the Rogers Park/West Ridge Historical Society, the Mexican Fine Arts Center, and the

Maxwell Street Preservation Society, largely because these organizations were in operation before the exhibition and they shared a similar mission with CHS. Though some community members complained that the formal relationships became more tenuous, others became actively involved in planning for another CHS exhibition, *Out of the Loop: Neighborhood Voices.*[32]

The goal of *Neighborhoods* was to tell the history of the neighborhood, not the history of one group. This meant discussing why things happened and not just celebrating what happened. It also meant taking a hard look at divisions, prejudices, and failures. As one curator succinctly explained, "History is not fun."[33] It is in this context that CHS staff found itself mired in a paradox. They wanted to collaborate with the community partners to get a more accurate story, but those partners had a vested interest in telling their own versions of history. Pushing for a more balanced interpretation threatened the collaboration; failure to do so risked sugarcoating the past. Instead of telling a more inclusive story, *Neighborhoods* told a different story. Similar to every interpretive program at CHS, or at any museum, the final product revealed little about the struggle over ownership of the past, only who won the right to tell the story. It was in the process, not in the final product, that the change occurred.

Instead of inviting community members to advise the staff, as so many museums have done, the CHS staff invited them to actually participate in the planning. Tracye Matthews deserves much of the credit for keeping CHS team members from taking over and making decisions without consulting the community partners. Her refusal to assert her authority to correct interpretations or to resolve specific issues—even to the point of letting the exhibition team fail—kept the community involved at every stage of the exhibitions' development. In the *Rogers Park* gallery guide, Scott La France argued that the "connections, dialogue, and learning the project has spawned among neighbors may, in fact, outweigh the final exhibition."[34] Success, then, should not be measured in the telling of the story but, rather, in how effectively the staff used the *Neighborhoods* project to challenge the society's interpretive practices.

As with *We the People* and the *Prologue for a New Century* biennial series, the *Neighborhoods* project changed how CHS collects and displays the city's history. Collecting, for much of the society's long past, had been focused on artifacts and manuscripts. With *Neighborhoods*, the staff became more conscious of the importance of using photography, tape recorders, and video cameras to document the changing urban landscape. In January 1996 Matthews and several staff members went down to the Near West Side and East Garfield Park, the fourth neighborhood, to document the closing of the Maxwell Street Market. Armed with cameras and videorecorders, they taped the demolition and interviewed residents about the event. They also collected signs and pieces of the sheds that had served as hot dog stands. This kind of foresight was a direct result of the collaborative process.

Neighborhoods also redefined the institution's relationship with its constituencies. Museums for their survival have always relied on outsiders, whose involvement has traditionally been limited to providing financial support, donating objects, serving on the board of trustees or auxiliary groups, or volunteering as gallery interpreters. Until *Neighborhoods,* visitors were seen as consumers of the society's products. They were invited into the institution, but they were not given the opportunity to participate in the interpretive process. In *Neighborhoods,* community members were welcomed as participants with a valuable kind of expertise. Where exhibitions in the past were intended to excite curiosity or to inspire awe and reverence, *Neighborhoods* generated discussion and debate with the goal of changing CHS from a temple into a forum—even if that debate was not reflected in the final exhibition.

The *Neighborhoods* project encouraged CHS to formalize its relationship with the community through two initiatives. The first initiative was the Community Advisory Council, formed in 1996 and composed of community, civic, education, and business leaders, some of whom were active in *Neighborhoods.* CAC served as a formal link between the museum and local communities, and although it remained active for only eighteen months, its purpose was to build upon the relationships that had been established in *Neighborhoods.* The second initiative involved the purchase of a one-hundred-thousand-square-foot building on State and Twenty-third streets in December 1999. The goal was to establish a presence close to the neighborhoods featured in the exhibition series. The mixed-use facility was intended mainly as a collection storage facility, which would also include a meeting and exhibition space. Unfortunately, CHS did not receive the state funds it had anticipated, and the future of the center remains in doubt. Both CAC and the State Street center reveal the practical problems of formalizing the institution's commitment to community history. These two initiatives have not had as much impact as the interpretive programs that followed.

The most important measure of the change that has taken place at CHS is to evaluate whether the sharing of power translated into other exhibition projects. In 1998 CHS applied for a second grant from the Joyce Foundation in order to continue reexamining the institution's civic role as the historian of Chicago. "My History Is Your History" was a project that initially had three components: curriculum material, multimedia resources in the form of Web sites and videos, and a learning center. Once the funding was received, the staff and community partners struggled to implement the original idea and ultimately decided to create another exhibition. This change did not alter the project's goal—to bring together diverse Chicagoans, many of whom were involved in the *Neighborhoods* project, to discuss their differences and commonalities—and simply allowed CHS to use the money to do what it does best—organize exhibitions.

Out of the Loop, which opened in February 2001 as a temporary component of the *Chicago History Galleries,* became the visible manifestation of the
project "My History Is Your History." Instead of highlighting single neighborhoods, *Out of the Loop* focused on what the four communities featured in
Neighborhoods had in common. Beginning in 1998 more than a hundred
neighborhood residents, many of whom had been active in *Neighborhoods,*
helped the CHS staff grapple with how to tell the story of Chicago since
World War II. The exhibition developer, John Russick, explained that the project
continued to rely upon the voices of individual experiences.[35] It did not use the
oral histories as evidence to support a historical argument, however; instead, the
voices become the argument itself. *Out of the Loop* was composed of a series of
perspectives from different community partners, which helped visitors understand not just what has happened since the war but what it means to those who
experienced it. To this end the exhibition team examined historical trends that
cut across community boundaries. In contrast to *Neighborhoods, Out of the Loop*
focused on highly charged topics such as class conflict, white flight (where
white middle-class residents fled the urban neighborhoods for more suburban
ones), and restrictive covenants (limits to the purchase or rental of real estate in
tended to discriminate against racial and ethnic groups). This critical approach
had not been possible in the four *Neighborhoods* exhibitions primarily because
they were part of the initial experiment. Once the community partners became
aware that CHS was dedicated to telling their stories in multiple venues, they became more willing to embrace less nostalgic interpretations.

The new focus helped the society to avoid ignoring broader historical
trends, a dilemma that often plagues local history exhibitions.[36] In contrast
to the 1979 *Chicago History Galleries* focus on the city's entrepreneurial spirit,
Out of the Loop integrated the experiences of different population groups that
had played a role in Chicago's development. This exhibition also subscribed
to historian Cary Carson's contested city model, an approach that analyzes
cities as places where more or less powerful groups of citizens advance competing urban visions.[37] *Out of the Loop* avoided presenting history as a series
of isolated experiences, which helped the institution and its constituencies
to understand how they are shaped by the larger urban process. This approach has helped guide the staff through reinstallation of the exhibits on
Chicago and American history.

For museums that are struggling on tight budgets and facing declining admissions, collaborative projects have become a last, best hope, applauded by
community groups, funders, and trustees. For CHS, *Neighborhoods* and *Out of
the Loop* both allowed the noncuratorial staff and the institution's varied constituencies to participate in important interpretive decisions. Even though, at
some level, the historians, designers, and educators functioned in their traditional roles, they were not the sole voices of authority. Community partners

proposed and vetoed themes, suggested layouts, selected artifacts, and helped organize public programs. CHS gave their lived experience legitimacy and authenticity in a way that had not been done before.

In this way the projects challenged the traditional culture of museums. Although these collaborations were all important first steps toward equalizing the conversation and interchange, Patricia Mooney-Melvin argues that there are limitations: "In the end, wherever there's a shared authority . . . it's not an equal share. At best it's two-thirds CHS and one-third the neighborhood. At its worst more like three-fourths or seven-eighths."[38] While museum professionals believe they are collaborating with local communities, in reality they are cooperating or coordinating.[39] Collaboration requires a transfer of authority, which is unlikely to happen at CHS or any other major history museum in the near future, not because the staff is unwilling to share power but because they work in a profession that requires expertise.

Experiments such as *Neighborhoods* may position constituencies as participants in an ongoing dialogue about cultural authority, but can they alter the status quo? The answer is no, unless museum professionals are prepared to question the historical consciousness that has given rise to the museum. Without careful attention to this issue, even the most innovative collaborations will fail to fully change the museum institution from a temple to a forum, because museums cannot relinquish full control over cultural capital and still consider themselves museums. Regardless of the extent of the inclusion proposed by collaborative projects, museum professionals still control who has the right to participate at the most basic level. And they should; they have the skills and experience to care for and interpret the artifacts that are important to the process of recording the past. Visitors rely on the professionals' expertise, and they come to such institutions with the expectation that the staff has something to teach and that something can be learned. As CHS has demonstrated, maintaining the professionals' position as the historians of the city of Chicago does not require that they practice their craft in isolation. This awareness, more than any other, is probably the most significant change to the institution since World War II.

The most important lesson to come out of the *Neighborhoods* projects has been an awareness that the complete sharing of authority is an unrealistic goal, in part because museums were not established for this purpose. While CHS staff members remain dedicated to the idea of cultural democracy, they also realize that museums cannot function without experts. However unpopular, power is an integral part of the museum endeavor. The institutions that understand this are the ones that reject romanticized notions of giving the power to the people, yet are willing to address the needs and expectations of disparate communities even in the face of conflict, controversy, and failure. *Neighborhoods* brought new constituencies into the temple to participate in a forum. Now CHS, as with all history museums, has to determine if this is enough.

CHAPTER SIX

Unfinished Business

[T]he forum is where the battles are fought, the temple is
where the victors rest. The former is a process, the latter is a product.

—DUNCAN F. CAMERON, "THE MUSEUM:

A TEMPLE OR THE FORUM" (1972)

Over the past century and a half, the staff, trustees, and
constituencies of CHS have transformed it into a new kind of civic institution. The building, research facilities, collections, galleries, and public programs have extended their reach to address a wider range of issues that are
more closely tied to current social, cultural, political, and economic concerns. The current institution barely resembles the historical society that ex-
isted in 1945 when Paul Angle became director, partly because claims to interpretive authority have changed in the interim. Where curators once
enjoyed nearly independent authority over the collections, in the 1980s they
began sharing their authority with academic scholars, designers, conservators, and educators. Since the 1990s, selected constituencies, energized by
culture wars and public debates over multiculturalism, have claimed that
they also should have input into the way CHS interprets their experiences;
the results have been seen in collaborative exhibitions and programs.
Change for any institution is slow, but it is especially complicated when
there are so few models from which to learn. CHS staff members deserve
credit for supporting what have been difficult, even controversial, choices.

There is no doubt that CHS has undergone a significant transformation
since its founding. Identifying change is one thing, measuring it quite another. There is very little quantifiable information about the institution apart
from attendance figures and employment statistics, and even these numbers
are problematic. Attendance figures do not provide enough detail to allow
any generalization about visitors' backgrounds, interests, and needs, or about

the quality of their experiences. Employment statistics document changes in salaries and staff demographics, but they are often incomplete and outdated. Audience surveys, an important part of museum evaluation process, have been conducted only sporadically at CHS, which makes reasonable comparisons difficult. In light of these limitations the only criteria available are by necessity more subjective. Innovations are temporary strategies in response to or in anticipation of a particular demand. In contrast, change disrupts categories of knowledge and challenges the current power structure. In order to offer a critical perspective on what might be called the institution's unfinished business, it is now necessary to move from the details of specific projects that sought to generate change to a more general survey of their long-term effects.

As a result of various factors—inventive exhibitions, a new management structure, recent renovations, the revised mission statement, the shift toward urban history, the growing visibility of the education department—CHS collections, exhibitions, and public programs now reflect greater diversity, audiences are more representative of the city's total population, and interpretive authority is more decentralized. CHS is no longer simply a storehouse for the collection but is, instead, a vital force that reaches out to both local and national constituencies. For most of its past, the staff's energy was focused on an elite group of visitors and donors, with very little attention given to the surrounding community. Traveling exhibitions, oral history projects, teacher-training workshops, the biennials, and the *Neighborhoods* project are all tangible illustrations that the institution is now fully committed to enlarging the role it plays in civic life. In 1982 one of the Scope Study consultants, Nicholas Westbrook, recommended that CHS develop a long-range plan to cooperate with the city's multiethnic populations, thus documenting and preserving the various histories of these groups. This undertaking would be accomplished not by "hauling it [history] off to Clark Street" but by offering "leadership and planning to ensure that the future's needs for the past are attended to for all sectors of the city's population."[1] Although the staff and consultants discussed collaboration as a necessary step in the interpretive process early in Ellsworth Brown's tenure, it did not become an institutional priority for another decade. Even though the collaborative process has limitations, it has succeeded in blurring the distinction between insiders and outsiders.

Social history, women's history, and urban history have all helped to legitimize the authority of memory and personal experience. As a result, what counts as expertise has become more contested within both society and the museum world in general. Collaborative projects focused on local histories illustrate this tension. For *City Comes of Age, Chicago Goes to War, Neighborhoods, Out of the Loop,* and *Teen Chicago,* CHS staff were beholden to local residents for artifacts, oral histories, resources, even approval. The planning of these exhibitions was as much a negotiation concerning access to individuals and collections as it was about interpreting the past. In this context the boundaries between insiders and outsiders became more fluid, and CHS adopted the role of facilitator. The society's demonstrated commitment to collaboration reveals that this new perspective is going to be the rule, rather than the exception.

Throughout the collaborative process CHS staff and trustees have learned an important lesson: that constituencies and museum professionals are not always interested in the same topics. Under Paul Angle, Clement Silvestro, and Harold Skramstad, curators proposed exhibitions that reflected internal interests and expertise. Ellsworth Brown, Douglas Greenberg, and Lonnie Bunch pushed the staff to present blockbuster shows that were popular with mainstream audiences and local history exhibitions that proved relevant to constituencies' everyday lives. Although it took CHS nearly five decades to become centered on the audience, the current exhibition schedule looks dramatically different from the schedule under Angle's tenure. This commitment to alter CHS's approach to exhibitions and programs showed a willingness to tackle difficult and potentially controversial issues. Two exhibitions that rose to this challenge have come from outside CHS.

Organized by the Jewish Museum in New York City, *Bridges and Boundaries: African Americans and American Jews* (April 7–July 4, 1994) explored the contentious relationships between African Americans and Jews in urban areas throughout the twentieth century. While CHS had addressed discrimination, violence, and racism in the past, this was the first exhibition to take a critical look at intragroup cooperation and intolerance. A traveling exhibition organized by the New York Public Library, *Long Road to Freedom: The Advocate History of the Gay and Lesbian Movement* (October 7–November 5, 1995), chronicled the history of gays and lesbians in America over the last quarter century. It represented the society's, and the city's, first attempt to deal with sexuality as a museum topic.

These and other exhibitions have attracted new constituencies. In the nineteenth and early twentieth centuries, CHS staff and visitors were virtually indistinguishable from each other.[2] They were drawn from the same social circles and had similar educational training and economic backgrounds. Even though the average CHS visitor is still white, middle-aged, and college-educated, the demographics are slowly changing, in part because of the society's outreach and interpretive programs. While different programs attract new constituencies, neighborhood tours and lectures focused on diversity do not necessarily attract larger ones. In fact, the institution's overall attendance numbers have decreased in the past decade: from 207,000 in 1990, to 159,000 in 1994, 144,603 in 1998, 168,759 in 2001, and 157,323 in 2003.[3]

Other large museums in Chicago—including the Shedd Aquarium, the Museum of Science and Industry, and the Art Institute of Chicago—also saw similar decreases. In some cases blockbuster exhibitions helped drive these figures up; for example, there was a 56 percent increase in attendance at exhibitions on Frida Kahlo and Diego Rivera at the Mexican Museum of Fine Arts in 2003. Even so, the overall numbers are declining.

Attendance figures obscure real change, however. Since the opening of the *Neighborhoods* project at CHS, the composition of the audience has begun to reflect the multicultural character of the neighborhoods on display. CHS is working on the assumption that its new approach will eventually help diversify its constituency. It is no longer enough to attract large crowds; a successful exhibition must attract a multicultural audience. This is not to say that the size of the audience is unimportant. In 2000 *Norman Rockwell: Pictures of the American People,* a traveling exhibition organized by the High Museum of Art in Atlanta and the Norman Rockwell Museum in Stockbridge, Massachusetts, opened to record crowds. While CHS is willing to experiment with *Neighborhoods* and *Teen Chicago,* a three-year project that resulted in an exhibition in 2004, they are also interested in creating an exhibition schedule that appeals to different audiences such as *Fashion, Flappers 'n All That Jazz* (2001) and *Chicago Sports! Ya Shoulda Been There* (2003).

The current institution advocates a nonprofit version of market segmentation, which involves the development of different products (in this case exhibitions and public programs) that appeal to different facets of the CHS audience.[4] The only difference between this strategy and the one used in the for-profit sector is that money is not the driving motivator. Rather, CHS hopes that market segmentation will encourage traditional visitors who are attracted to exhibitions on Abraham Lincoln and Norman Rockwell to take the time to tour the museum's less conventional interpretations.

While the programs and initiatives of the past several decades have redefined the relationship between CHS and its constituency, it is important to evaluate the extent to which they have affected power relations within the institution, itself. Change in museums, as with any large organization, is laborious. Most of the initiatives sponsored by CHS in the past decade have been based upon a relatively simple argument—multicultural constituencies will attend programs and exhibitions that focus on their specific histories. Audience studies tell a different story, however.

In their survey of visitors at European art museums, Pierre Bourdieu and Alain Darbel explain that the number of people visiting museums increases markedly with an increasing level of education.[5] Although race, gender, and class might be mitigating forces, they are not independent variables. Race, a key feature in the museum world's definition of multiculturalism, is an unreliable variable in predicting museumgoing behavior.[6] Thus programs, initiatives, and exhibitions that presume a direct correlation between race and participation and are marketed accordingly are bound to have limited appeal. Instead, museum professionals should broaden the conception of difference to recognize that homogeneous communities do not exist and that other factors, including gender, religion, age, leisure preference, class, sexuality, and education are equally important variables. This broadening of the conception of difference requires that museum professionals consider their constituencies' lives in broader community contexts and also demands that they go one step further, to examine how their institution presents invisible barriers to visitation.[7]

The best way to judge how much a museum values its visitors is to evaluate how their needs are met. CHS does not pose burdensome financial or social constraints on its constituencies. The admission fee is five dollars for adults, three dollars for senior citizens and students, one dollar for children aged between six and twelve, and there are no specific dress codes. But there are more subtle barriers to visitation.[8] For example, although CHS does produce brochures or maps that are in Spanish, this ignores that a large percentage of tourists are often from China, Japan, and the Philippines. Additionally, a significant number of new immigrants, according to the 2000 census, are from India, Poland, and the former Soviet Union.[9] Label copy is rarely bilingual, which is surprising in light of the resources that have been directed over the past decade at both programs and exhibitions aimed at attracting diverse audiences. While the education department occasionally produces large-print labels, none of the installations provide cassette recordings, touch tours, sign-interpreted lectures, or special tours for the learning impaired.[10] Wheelchair access, available for the building and for most of the galleries, is the main arena in which CHS complies with the requirements of the Americans with Disabilities Act. But wheelchair users compose a very small proportion of the disabled population. Seating in the galleries is also limited, making it difficult for elderly visitors to comfortably view exhibitions. Finally, the rhetoric of inclusion is at odds with the revenue-generating aspects of the society. The café and to a lesser degree the bookstore are expensive, which essentially means that disadvantaged audiences are denied access to an important part of the museum experience.

Multiculturalism, as it is currently conceived in museums, has had the unexpected result of silencing critical interpretations of marginalized communities. This became an issue regarding an exhibition that CHS actually never mounted. Its absence reveals as much about interpretive authority as anything on display. While interpretations of overt forms of discrimination between communities have become commonplace at CHS, one curator learned that investigating conflict within those communities is more problematic.

During his tenure as curator of prints and photographs, Larry Viskochil collaborated with local photographers on a series of contemporary photographic studies, and half a dozen exhibitions resulted from these collaborations. These innovative partnerships encouraged twentieth-century collecting, strengthened the bond between CHS and local artists, and served as a model for other museums. While working on *Changing Chicago: Public Rituals and Diversions* (April 22–July 31, 1989), Viskochil became interested in the photographs of Lloyd DeGrane. Several of DeGrane's contributions to *Changing Chicago* featured Stateville Prison inmates as their subject. After the exhibition closed, Viskochil approached DeGrane with the idea of documenting life in the prison for another exhibition. Established in 1925, Stateville is in Joliet, Illinois, about one hour from Chicago, and it is one of the largest maximum-security prisons in the United States. As with most such institutions serving urban areas, African Americans and Latinos are overrepresented among the inmate population. Viskochil argued that because of its proximity to the city and its large population of Chicagoans, it was a neighborhood of young Chicago men and thus worthy of documentation.

Between 1989 and 1994 DeGrane photographed the prison and its inmates and kept in close contact with CHS. Despite his vigorous efforts, Viskochil was unable to raise the necessary funds, partly because of a lack of support from the development office and partly because of the controversial and provocative nature of the subject matter. The images depicted the most violent and humiliating aspects of prison life: handmade weapons, profanity and pornography on the walls, inmates with tattoos and scars, filth, and loneliness. Although painful to view, Viskochil reasoned that such candid portrayals of these issues might make visitors more aware of the problems of prison life and more reluctant to accept the "three strikes you're out" approach to punishment.

Most of CHS staff opposed the idea, however. In a very tense meeting with Viskochil and members of the education department, several staff educators complained that the show was underdeveloped, the images too powerful, and that it would be difficult to integrate them into the existing CHS curriculum. Others argued that representations of African Americans and Latinos that were not positive and uplifting should never be shown at CHS. Without funding or institutional support, the exhibition was never mounted. Several of DeGrane's photographs originally intended for the CHS exhibition were ultimately integrated into *Discipline and Photograph,* an exhibition on prisons curated by James R. Hugunin, on view at the Peace Museum from September to November 1996. But its failure at CHS revealed "what is possible and what is not possible in the 1990s."[11]

Despite the rhetoric of inclusion, controversial topics have always been a problem for museums.[12] While CHS has taken important strides toward presenting a more accurate history, additional attention to more troublesome topics, some of which were addressed in *Out of the Loop,* would help make the society more relevant to the lives of individuals in its constituencies. While museum professionals should keep pushing at the interpretive boundaries, it is important to note that there are very real risks involved. Museum professionals who propose controversial subjects have a difficult time finding funders. At CHS the staff had trouble raising money for *Bridges and Boundaries* (a traveling exhibit that CHS hosted), and Douglas Greenberg warned the board of trustees "to be aware of the possibility of significant and possibly negative coverage of the exhibit in the press."[13]

From a national perspective, the controversies over contemporary art and the *Enola Gay,* for example, made sponsors and trustees reluctant to attach their names to volatile topics. Curators, afraid of losing their jobs, have come to accept that there are limits to what can be presented, and for good reason. The curator responsible for mounting *Robert Mapplethorpe: The Perfect Moment* was put on trial for obscenity. Martin Harwitt, former director of the National Air and Space Museum, was fired over *The Last Act: The Atomic Bomb and the End of World War II,* and the museum subsequently canceled its exhibition on Vietnam for fear of retaliation. Another casualty of the culture wars, Marion Casey, resigned amid controversy over the community's role in the City Museum of New York's *Gaelic Gotham: A History of the Irish in New York.* Although Alfred Young, curator of *We the People,* proposed a "Bill of Rights for Museums" to insulate museum professionals from such attacks, the bill has not had much impact, partly because constituencies do not believe that museums deserve special protection.[14]

In the current climate, museum professionals, like politicians, are viewed as public figures open to scrutiny, criticism, and censure. Museums are not universities, their constituencies are not students, and visitors do not necessarily go to museums to have their ideas and belief systems challenged. Many constituencies believe that museums should be divorced from the mundane experiences of everyday life and used as a kind of national currency to symbolize social and cultural prestige.[15] Using this logic, museums have a responsibility to purge history of conflict and distill it down to a narrative of progress and triumph.[16]

While most museum professionals claim that museums have always been highly politicized spaces, their constituencies often expect them to be above such conflict. For many, museums function as ritual sites where visitors are expected to exercise their civic pride.[17] Museums that try to expose the power of that cultural sign by bringing the forum inside the temple also ask their patrons to take a more critical view of the past, something the latter are seldom willing to do. This impasse, more than any other issue, might explain why real change in museums seems so fleeting. Despite all the efforts detailed in this book, assumptions and expectations about museums ultimately undermine any significant challenge to authority. This is not to say that museum professionals should abandon their efforts but, rather, that they should understand and appreciate their constituencies' assumptions and expectations.

The desire to make reparations to previously marginalized groups by mainstreaming their history seems a noble idea. But museums are not social service agencies and at this stage in their development are not equipped to do much more than acknowledge injustice, which is not in and of itself a heroic act. Heroism requires a different kind of commitment, a commitment that would begin with an evaluation of the internal policies of the institution. The rhetoric of multiculturalism does not always translate into changed operations, and there are areas that continue to undermine the society's commitment to inclusiveness and fairness. The goal of this discussion is not to expose the shortcomings of CHS but rather to demonstrate that, unless change permeates every facet of the museum's operations, change will always be modest.

The staff responsible for the interpretive programs at CHS have been trained in colleges and universities, and with some notable exceptions they are white and middle-class. This is mainly because the fields of public history, museum studies, American studies, and art history do not typically attract minority students.[18] The minority staff members that CHS does employ are overrepresented in clerical, janitorial, and other low-paying positions such as security and education. These demographic trends are consistent with mainstream museums throughout the nation, in most of which over 90 percent of staff members responsible for interpretation are white, and women and people of color are seldom in positions of authority.[19] This is partly why the presence of Lonnie Bunch at CHS is so important. He is the first and only African American director of a major museum in Chicago.

Remedying this statistical imbalance through hiring is only a partial solution. Another dimension shaping this issue is the amount of education required for specific positions and the ways in which invisible barriers restrict access to this training. Permanent change in museums will require radical change in the educational system. A more pragmatic option for museums in the short term is to consider hiring individuals who, although perhaps lacking in traditional training, are familiar with the histories and experiences of underserved communities and who have the requisite skills to succeed in an environment of collaboration and shared authority. While this is an intriguing solution, it is impossible to ignore that such individuals would be lacking in the skills essential for the care, safety, and interpretation of the collections. The solution, then, might be best conceived as a compromise. To the current staff of traditionally trained conservators, educators, curators, and designers could be added local artists and community activists. While this approach would validate the new kinds of expertise that were so valued in

Neighborhoods and subsequent collaborative projects, it also raises two complicated questions: Does the hiring of a few community representatives make the process of interpretation more democratic? Would such a strategy alienate the very professionals who help the institution function?

Some museum professionals argue that, just as they finally succeed in transforming their institutions from amateur to professional organizations, they are suddenly asked to abandon their newly adopted standards. This is a legitimate concern. The consultants, academic historians, and community partners who collaborated with CHS in the past three decades revealed that museum work requires very specific skills that are essential to the conservation, preservation, and interpretation of the collections. But valuing new kinds of expertise might offer added benefits. While bringing outsiders into the museum would require additional training, it also would provide museums with new sources of talent that otherwise would be overlooked because of the lack of traditional, academic credentials.[20]

Diversity is also an issue for the board of trustees. For most of the society's lifetime, the board was comprised of wealthy white men—and occasionally their wives—from prominent Chicago families. Over the past two decades, progressive board members and CHS staff have worked to make the board less exclusive. They replaced old money with new by appointing local business people from a variety of professions. In 1990 a professor at Lake Forest College, Michael Ebner, was asked to join the board, and he was the first academic historian to serve in this capacity. More women and African Americans now serve on the board, which helps the society's employment and governance policies reflect their potential user groups.

In the past decade CHS has taken steps toward making the whole institution, not just its interpretive programs, more democratic. The reorganizations under Douglas Greenberg and Lonnie Bunch recognized that institutional success depends on a more heterogeneous blend of specialists with different, but complementary, skills. Despite occasional setbacks, the staff members continue to think imaginatively about how best to involve their constituencies in dialogues concerning what counts as history. This approach, combined with a willingness to question the organizational traditions upon which the society was founded, is the measure of the society's success.

Epilogue

On October 4, 2003, CHS opened *Harold Washington: The Man and the Movement,* profiling Chicago's first black mayor on the twentieth anniversary of his election. Featuring photographs, political and personal artifacts, and video presentations, the exhibition analyzed Washington's leadership style and the multiethnic coalition that helped elect him in 1983. "In essence, Harold opened the door that you can't shut," said Lonnie Bunch, the current president of CHS. "These folks now have a piece in every government, and I don't think you'll ever see a government in Chicago that will reflect the way the city was before Harold."[1]

This exhibition serves as an apt metaphor for CHS itself. The shift to social and urban history, the questioning of authority both inside and outside the institution, and the appointment of the first African American president, opened a door that cannot be shut. CHS will never again be the institution that the twelve founders hoped would preserve a patriotic past in perpetuity for an elite few.

CHS was established as a private, nonprofit corporation by a group of citizens who loved history and wanted to preserve it for future generations. When the founders met on that spring day in 1856 in the law office of Scammon and McCagg, they made their purpose public, as reflected in CHS's first mission statement—"to encourage historical enquiry and spread historical information, especially within the State of Illinois, and also within the entire territory of the North-West." This mission along with nearly everything else about CHS has changed in the century and a half since.[2]

Perhaps the best way to end this study is to return to the beginning. Since the 1970s, museums and their constituencies, with some notable exceptions, have largely embraced Duncan Cameron's assumption that museums should not be sites of unquestioning authority (such as temples) but should instead become places of confrontation, experimentation, and debate (such as forums). Although largely rejecting a focus on confrontation, CHS has both reflected and been at the forefront of this trend. It is a different institution as a result. Yet the question remains: Where does the future lie?

The answer may be linked with a man from Belleville, New Jersey, who recalls that at the age of five he saw a photograph of a group of children with a caption that read "anonymous." Lonnie Griffin Bunch Sr., the child's grandfather, asked, "Isn't it a shame that people could live their lives, die, and just be known as anonymous?" That moment helped convince the young boy to dedicate his career "to give voice to the anonymous."[3]

At the age of forty-seven, after ten years at the Smithsonian, Lonnie Bunch took the helm at CHS in 2001. Of all the institution's directors he has the most diverse range of experience. His grandfather was a sharecropper who put himself through college and received a degree in dentistry at Howard University before World War I. When the state of New Jersey refused to accept the degree, Lonnie Griffin Bunch Sr. went to graduate school a second time, at the University of Chicago, and finally opened his practice. His grandson, Lonnie, was educated at Howard and American universities, and began his career as an education specialist at the Smithsonian's National Air and Space Museum and as an adjunct lecturer at American University in 1978. The next year he became an assistant professor of American and Afro-American history at the University of Massachusetts Dartmouth, then he joined the faculty at Packer Collegiate Institute in Brooklyn. Leaving academia, he moved from Brooklyn to Los Angeles to help establish and to work as a curator at the California African American Museum, a position he held until he joined the Smithsonian as supervising curator of the National Museum of American History in 1989. Blending his talents as a museum educator, curator, and academic historian, Bunch moved to CHS with the goal of making it "the model for all history museums, not only in the country, but [in] the world."[4]

He was poised to do just that. When Bunch came to Chicago, the worldwide museum community was optimistic about a bright future. The falling attendance numbers and funding crisis of the early 1990s seemed to be over. Dozens of articles appeared in magazines and newspapers with headlines such as "Museum Attendance on the Rise," "And Still the Crowds Come," and "Blockbuster Shows Lure Record Crowds into U.S. Museums."[5] Large exhibitions were attracting thousands of visitors, and museums were responding to the forecasts by planning bigger and better shows. In 1999 *Monet in the 20th Century* drew 565,992 visitors during its three-month run at the Museum of Fine Arts in Boston. A year later, when London's Royal Academy hosted the same exhibition, the visitors numbered 739,324.[6] The *New York Times* reported that in 2000, "21 exhibitions in the United States lured more than

200,000 visitors each into museums, including those in Minneapolis, Brooklyn, St. Louis, and Philadelphia."[7] In comparison, in 1996, only fourteen exhibitions had drawn similar crowds. Also in 2000, the National Gallery in Athens, Greece, reported that *El Greco: Identity and Transformation* attracted 629,572 visitors, and the Los Angeles County Museum of Art counted 821,004 at *Van Gogh's van Goghs*.[8] It was an exciting time, when statistics—"one in every 28 Americans is a member of at least one museum" and "museums in this country average 865 million visitors a year"—were reported with glee.[9]

Although most of the exhibitions attracting these kinds of numbers were to be found in art museums, history museums were not far behind. In keeping with the trend, CHS opened two large traveling shows in 2000, *Treasures of Mount Vernon: George Washington Revealed* and *Norman Rockwell: Pictures of the American People*. *Fashion, Flappers 'n All That Jazz*, an exhibition drawn from the society's extensive costume collection, opened in fall 2001. CHS added *The American Presidency: A Glorious Burden*, a traveling version of the NMAH exhibition co-curated by Bunch, to the exhibition calendar for 2002.

Then everything changed. Nine months after Bunch began his tenure, events of September 11, 2001, forced museums to reevaluate their missions and rethink their relationships to their audiences. CHS, along with many cultural institutions throughout the nation, struggled to make sense of the tragedy. Recent trends in the museum world, with the focus on community building and civic engagement, prepared them for this new role.

When, in 1998, the American Association of Museums had launched the "Museums and Communities Initiative," museums embraced the opportunity to "discuss creative strategies for effective community-museum engagement."[10] In late 2000 and early 2001, AAM sponsored six dialogues with educators, elected officials, community activists, and museum leaders in six cities: Providence, Tampa, Los Angeles, Detroit, Wichita, and Bellingham, Washington. Many of the issues raised seemed mostly theoretical until September 11. In the aftermath of the attack, dozens of museums sought to address the complexity of the historic moment. Now the focus of the AAM's initiative was to encourage "museums to pursue their potential as active, visible players in community life."[11] Terrorism provided museums with an opportunity to determine how much they mattered when that community life was threatened.

The immediate role played by museums after the September 11 attacks depended upon their proximity to the disaster. Museums in Manhattan became makeshift hospitals, barracks, and social service agencies. The Lower East Side Tenement Museum provided food, water, and medical assistance to those fleeing the disaster site of the World Trade Center. The Liberty Science Center became a staging area for emergency-management personnel, police, and victims. The National Museum of the American Indian's Heye Center housed soldiers involved in the rescue efforts.[12] All served as safe havens.

Although not as immediately affected, museums around the country responded quickly. The Field Museum in Chicago offered free admission; produced a play called *Surviving Violence;* organized special programs related to the exhibition *Living Together,* which focused on cultural diversity; and held town-hall meetings on September 15, 16, and 22. The Field Museum encouraged visitors to use their museum as a gathering place to help put the tragedy in historical perspective.[13] The manager for performing arts and lectures, Encarnacion Teruel, explained the museum's approach: "the museum's role is to provide people with information and resources to educate themselves to better understand the world that we live in. Public spaces like museums are unique spaces . . . . You may have people coming into this museum with different opinions, but because of the structure of the public space, they realize that this is a forum for coexisting and compromising."[14]

Dozens of institutions organized similar discussions, including three museums in Pennsylvania: the Historical Society of Pennsylvania, which hosted "Echoes and Reflections: Learning from Ethnic Strife in Times of National Crisis"; the Independence Seaport Museum, which hosted "America as a Super Power: 100 Years Ago and Today"; and the Chester County Historical Society, which hosted a three-part series on Islam, the press, and civil liberties entitled "A Nation Challenged: Perspectives on September 11."[15] In Los Angeles, the Japanese American National Museum organized programs that focused on connections between the U.S. internment of Japanese residents during World War II and recent examples of discrimination against Arab Americans.

CHS joined the group and hosted "September 11th: Reflections on a Changed America," which drew together journalists, civil libertarians, and author Studs Terkel.[16] On the first anniversary of the event, CHS opened *New York September 11th by Magnum Photographers,* a traveling exhibition organized by the New-York Historical Society. To coincide with this exhibition, Chicago-area schoolchildren devised a variety of ways to commemorate the tragedy, and some of their efforts were on display in the CHS lobby. The Latin School's High Jump Program created the High Jump Flag, comprised of 240 squares symbolizing themes such as home, community, and security. Hitch Elementary School made the Hitch Quilt out of 370 cardboard squares. Resurrection Catholic Academy created an ofrenda (altar) to remember the victims.[17] All of these programs and exhibitions suggest, according to Lonnie Bunch, that museums can be "helpful tools for people wrestling with despair and uncertainty"—not by skirting controversy, but by offering opportunities for discussion and reflection.[18]

The events organized around the tragedy also suggest a changed environment for cultural institutions. When *We the People: Creating a New Nation, 1765–1820* opened at CHS in 1987, the bicentennial year of the signing of the U.S. Constitution, uncritical celebrations abounded. Few of those programs analyzed the heated debates that had taken place concerning how to govern the new nation. Indeed, the Commission on the Bicentennial of the U.S. Constitution led by Warren Burger focused almost exclusively on pageantry and patriotism. CHS took a radically different approach and examined the roles that women, founders, farmers, indentured servants, Native Americans, African Americans (both enslaved and free), and others, all played in shaping the new nation. The exhibition gave audiences a new understanding of the founding period, just as the programs organized by many museums after September 11 sought to offer new perspectives on terrorism, tolerance, stereotyping, civil liberties, and religious fundamentalism. In 1987 CHS was nearly alone in the wilderness; in 2001 it was one voice among many. Throughout its lifetime CHS has both blazed trails and reflected trends.

The question, however, remains: Will the very real costs of September 11 turn back the clock? Will funders, suffering from a weakened economy, shy away from experimental, potentially controversial subjects and opt instead for conventional, well-worn interpretations? Will programs addressing racism, sexism, and other forms of discrimination be labeled unpatriotic? In the past three decades CHS and other history museums have done a lot of good work in order to connect with their communities; will this work help them survive?

CHS and museums around the country face significant challenges that had emerged long before, yet were exacerbated by, the tragedy. Museums face increased competition from sporting events, shopping malls, television, the internet, amusement parks, and movie theaters, while a decline in tourism further reduces revenue. To complicate matters, CHS operates in one of the most competitive markets for museums in the nation. Bunch explained: "The attacks of September 11 contributed mightily to the downturn in the American economy, now officially recognized as a recession, and have led to a decline in tourism, decreased tax revenues, and the continuing downward slide of the stock market."[19] All of these trends have negatively affected attendance figures that only a year or two before had been reported so optimistically.

In contrast to the coverage of museums in the late 1990s, articles in 2002 and 2003 now had anxious headlines such as "New York Arts Being Cut Back in Money Pinch," and "Deep Cuts: The Crisis in State Funding." Randall Bourscheidt, president for the Alliance for the Arts in New York City, summed up the overall feeling among the museum and arts communities: "It's like a patient whose health is slipping." The Smithsonian reported a 38 percent drop in attendance in 2002, the Guggenheim a 50 percent reduction, and the Shedd Aquarium a 35 percent loss. The resulting layoffs, exhibition and program cancellations, tour group cancellations, and fiscal tightening indicate a period of retrenchment for museums that threatens to reverse decades of innovation and change.[20]

Despite the dire news, CHS is poised to survive and even thrive, partly because it has been flexible enough to change over the years, thus ensuring sustainability. Even though admissions have declined in recent years and there has been a 15 percent reduction in staff as a result of a hiring freeze and a small number of layoffs, CHS announced in September 2003 that it was planning a significant renovation.[21] Before Douglas Greenberg left, the institution had raised twelve million dollars to fund the project. The entire budget will be closer to twenty million, and the staff and trustees are currently engaged in a campaign that they anticipate will be a success.

The changes will be extensive. On the second floor, *We the People, A House Divided,* the Costume Alcoves, and *Out of the Loop* will be dismantled, and a six-thousand-square-foot rental space that encompasses the 1932 lobby and overlooks the park will be added to the east side. This change reflects a broader trend in the field that places greater emphasis on earned revenue. The south side of the second floor will feature the new *Chicago History Galleries,* at sixteen thousand square feet the largest exhibition in the society. The north side will include the new American history wing. Elements of *We the People* and *A House Divided* will be integrated into a combined exhibition that will also include more materials on the Jacksonian era. A second exhibition that moves the story into the twentieth century is slated to open later in the decade. Additionally, there will be a sixty-five-hundred-square-foot gallery dedicated to temporary exhibitions. The main staircase on the first floor will be removed and the lobby completely renovated to showcase the soaring ceiling. A new costume and textile gallery will be added. *Hands on History* will be retooled and made more interactive, providing an immersive experience that more closely resembles the approach taken by children's museums over the past several decades. A "Greatest Hits" trail will draw visitors through the first floor to allow them to view the society's signature artifacts.

One of the most significant changes is the renewed emphasis on national history collecting, reflected in the new Lincoln exhibition. *Pioneer Life,* a gallery that opened in 1973, has been dismantled in anticipation of a permanent exhibition focused on the life and times of Abraham Lincoln. Although the original letter has not survived, on January 18, 1861, CHS secretary and librarian William Barry invited Lincoln to become a CHS member. In April 2002 CHS purchased from Christie's a presidential order from Lincoln to secretary of state William H. Seward asking him to affix the seal of the United States of America to the Emancipation Proclamation. This complements the society's already extensive holdings, which include a gold monogrammed watch presented to Lincoln by the *Springfield State Journal,* the silk and beaver top hat he wore to his inauguration, and his famous dispatch to General Grant as the Union forces pursued Robert E. Lee's Army of Northern Virginia. CHS will continue to build the collection and plans to collaborate with the

Lincoln Presidential Library and Museum in Springfield, Illinois. As one CHS trustee explained, "Lincoln is our Sue," in reference to the Field Museum's iconic Tyrannosaurus rex skeleton called Sue, suggesting that Lincoln's legacy is a significant yet underutilized part of CHS's brand.[22] This might seem like an unusual shift for an institution that in 1977 made a philosophical commitment to local history. The return to national history, though, does not come at the expense of presenting and preserving Chicago's past. For the first time in its lifetime, the institution's collections are rich enough, and the staff is sufficiently prepared, to do both.

The Lincoln exhibition might be best juxtaposed to *Teen Chicago,* a three-year initiative focused on how teenagers have affected Chicago's history in the twentieth century. This was funded in part by the Joyce Foundation and the NEH. Tracye Matthews, who coordinated *Neighborhoods,* returned to CHS to work on this collaborative project. Borrowing from the *Neighborhoods* model, a Teen Council comprised of a diverse group of fifteen teenagers was employed by the museum to conduct cross-generational oral histories in order to explore the changing nature of teenage life in an urban setting. The research resulted in a major exhibition that opened on April 18, 2004, and proved to be an imaginative way to attract an audience that all history museums want. Further in the future, CHS is planning an exhibition on Catholic Chicago, again drawing on the *Neighborhoods* model of community collaboration, but conceiving of the neighborhood as a spiritual rather than a physical place.

One of the most ambitious projects focuses on the lesbian, gay, bisexual, and transgendered community. Working with an advisory board that includes George Chauncey, a professor at the University of Chicago and author of (among other titles) *Gay New York: Gender, Urban Culture, and the Making of the Gay Male World, 1890–1940,* CHS has fostered an ongoing partnership with the community to create educational programs. In the next several years, the institution plans to develop a major exhibition on a topic that has largely been ignored by museums.[23] In 1995 CHS hosted *Long Road to Freedom: The Advocate History of the Gay and Lesbian Movement,* a traveling exhibition organized by the New York Public Library, even though it did not focus on Chicago's experience. Although some constituencies have questioned the legitimacy of this enterprise, the institution has made a firm commitment to diversity in all forms, again paving the way.

To predict the future of CHS, it is important to evaluate recent trends in the funding climate and the changing demographics of visitors and donors. Over the past three decades, museum donor demographics have shifted dramatically. The traditional middle-aged white male is no longer the most important donor.[24] CHS has been planning for this eventuality since Clement Silvestro's tenure in the early 1960s. The new donors are a diverse lot, including women, baby boomers from all racial and ethnic backgrounds who were mainly educated during the civil rights movement, and the young, newly wealthy (though the dot.com bust has significantly reduced the size of the last group). The next generation also has different expectations; in an era of corporate scandals and diminishing resources, members of the next generation are demanding accountability and transparency.[25] They are not Philip Wrigley, Marshall Field, or William McCormick Blair, the old-style donors who were content simply to write a check over lunch without asking too many questions. New generation donors are scrutinizing institutional policies and operations, insisting as a condition of their support that organizations adhere to a business plan in order to ensure a solid return on their investment.[26] Even a cursory glance at CHS's programming over the past three decades shows that the institution has addressed many of the concerns of this varied group, building credibility that has translated into support and long-term relationships. CHS has, as Bunch explained in a speech given to the Joyce Foundation board of directors in 2002, embraced diversity as being central to institutional success.[27]

Many state-run historical societies and organizations face budget cuts, whereas, as a private institution, CHS's proactive decision to diversify its funding sources has paid off. In contrast to its counterparts in Minnesota, New Jersey, Texas, Washington, South Carolina, and Arizona, CHS has not suffered dramatic cuts in funding or large-scale layoffs. The national climate has impacted the field, however. The Massachusetts Historical Commission budget was severely cut; in 2003 the Wisconsin Historical Society eliminated thirty positions; in 2004 the Minnesota Historical Society faced a 16 percent reduction in state support.[28] These institutions have to determine how to expand their offerings in order to continue serving a diverse constituency during these lean years. The boom is over, but the demands placed by communities on museums will not abate. Retrenchment is not an option, as changing demographics show. By the year 2010, for example, Latinos will comprise the single largest ethnic group in the United States, and few mainstream institutions have as yet interpreted the U.S. Latino experience.[29]

Although funding, demographics, and attendance are significant issues, they are, as September 11 so poignantly demonstrated, only part of the story. I want to end with an observation made by *New York Times* art critic Michael Kimmelman. In August 2001 he attended a meeting where art directors and curators in Austria were boasting about increased attendance at their institutions. Kimmelman, however, noted that "the question that hung in the air was, money aside, to what end?"[30] The end, in the case of CHS, seems to be to make the museum not only into a forum for dialogue and experimentation but into a place that is truly useful and relevant to all its stakeholders—the staff, trustees, members, public, and donors—as they try to make sense of history and of the place each one holds in it.

Notes

INTRODUCTION: FROM TEMPLE TO FORUM

1. D'Amato quoted in Richard Bolton, ed., *Culture Wars: Documents from Recent Controversies in the Arts* (New York; New Press, 1992), 3; Boorstin quoted in Edward J. Sozanski, "View of the West Raises Hackles in Congress," *Philadelphia Inquirer*, 16 June 1991, F1.

2. Mike Wallace, *Mickey Mouse History and Other Essays on American Memory* (Philadelphia: Temple University Press, 1996), 292 (quotation), 298. Public Law 101-121 was attached to an appropriations bill that provided the NEA and NEH with their annual budgets. The final statute was based on *Miller v. California* and stands as the legal definition of obscenity. It included the final version of the Helms amendment that denied funding to "indecent" programs. "None of the funds authorized to be appropriated for the National Endowment for the Arts or the National Endowment for the Humanities may be used to promote, disseminate, or produce materials which . . . may be considered obscene, including but not limited to, depictions of sadomasochism, homoeroticism, the sexual exploitation of children, or individuals engaged in sex acts and which, when taken as a whole, do not have serious literary, artistic, political, or scientific value." Excerpt from Public Law 101-121, 101st Congress, October 23, 1989, quoted in Bolton, *Culture Wars*, 121.

3. Wallace, *Mickey Mouse History*, 297 (Will quoted, 299).

4. Theodore Low, *The Museum as a Social Instrument: A Study Undertaken for the Committee on Education of the American Association of Museums* (New York: Metropolitan Museum of Art, 1942), 24.

5. Duncan Cameron, "The Museum: A Temple or the Forum," *Journal of World History* 14.1 (1972): 197–210.

6. See Maurice Berger, "Are Art Museums Racist?" *Art in America* 68 (September 1990): 69–76; Ivan Karp, Christine Kraemer, and Steven D. Lavine, eds., *Museums and Communities: The Politics of Public Culture* (Washington, DC: Smithsonian Institution Press, 1992); Ivan Karp and Steven D. Lavine, eds., *Exhibiting Cultures: The Poetics and Politics of Museum Display* (Washington, DC: Smithsonian Institution Press, 1991); Steven Lavine, "Museums and Multiculturalism: Who Has Control?" *Museum News* 68 (March/April 1989): 34–36; Barbara Franco, "Doing History in Public: Balancing Historical

Fact with Public Meaning," *Perspectives* (May/June 1995): 5–8; Barbara Franco, "The History Museum Curator of the 21st Century," *History News* (Summer 1996): 6–10; Barbara Franco, "The Communication Conundrum: What Is the Message? Who Is Listening?" *Journal of American History* 81 (June 1994): 151–63; Wallace, *Mickey Mouse History;* Robert Archibald, *A Place to Remember: Using History to Build Community* (Walnut Creek, CA: AltaMira Press, 1999); American Association of Museums, *Mastering Civic Engagement: A Challenge to Museums* (Washington, DC: American Association of Museums, 2002); Warren Leon and Roy Rosenzweig, eds., *History Museums in the United States: A Critical Assessment* (Urbana: University of Illinois Press, 1989).

7. S. Dillon Ripley, *The Sacred Grove: Essays on Museums* (New York: Simon and Schuster, 1969); Robert McCormack Adams, "Smithsonian Horizons," *Smithsonian* 23 (April 1992): 13.

8. Susan Hegeman makes these important distinctions in "Shopping for Identities: *A Nation of Nations* and the Weak Ethnicity of Objects," *Public Culture* 3 (Spring 1991): 76.

9. Terence Turner, "Anthropology and Multiculturalism: What Is Anthropology that Multiculturalists Should Be Mindful of It?" *Cultural Anthropology* 8 (November 1993): 413–14. Turner further differentiates between two kinds of multiculturalism. Critical multiculturalism uses cultural diversity as "a basis for challenging, revising, and revitalizing basic notions and principles common to dominant and minority cultures alike, so as to construct a more vital, open, and democratic common culture," whereas difference multiculturalism reduces culture to a "tag for ethnic identity and a license for political and intellectual separatism" (413–14).

10. Robert R. Janes makes this point in *Museums and the Paradox of Change: A Case Study in Urgent Adaptation* (Calgary: Glenbow Museum, 1995), 18.

11. The terms *visitors, audiences,* and *members* describe specific population groups. The term *constituency* allows for a discussion of these groups as collectivities and also includes individuals who may have never set foot in a museum but who still claim authority to comment on its practices and programs. *Constituency* implies some degree of power. In politics it is the vote, while in museums it is the ability to scrutinize and question policy, and in limited cases to institute change.

12. For a more detailed discussion of the evolving role of museum curators see Barbara Franco's "Panel commentary" in Bryant F. Tolles, ed., *Museum Curatorship: Rhetoric vs. Reality* (Newark: University of Delaware, 1987), 45.

13. Gaynor Kavanagh, *History Curatorship* (Washington, DC: Smithsonian Press, 1990), 11; Janes, *Museums,* 148.

14. Eilean Hooper-Greenhill, "Counting Visitors or Visitors Who Count?" in Robert Lumley, ed., *The Museum Time Machine* (New York: Routledge, 1988), 223.

15. Franco, "Panel commentary," 44; Franco, "History Museum Curator," 10.

16. Carolyn P. Blackmon, Teresa K. LaMaster, Lisa C. Roberts, and Beverly Serrell, *Open Conversations: Strategies for Professional Development in Museums* (Chicago: Department of Education, Field Museum of Natural History, 1988), 67.

1: DECADES OF CHANGE

1. Paul Angle, "The Chicago Historical Society, 1856–1946," *Chicago History* 1 (Fall 1945–Summer 1948): 58.

2. Robert L. Brubaker, "The Development of an Urban History Research Center: The Chicago Historical Society," *Chicago History* 7 (Spring 1978): 24.

3. Ibid., 25.

4. Byron York, "The Pursuit of Culture: Founding the Chicago Historical Society, 1856," *Chicago History* (Fall 1981): 175.

5. David R. Brigham, *Public Culture in the Early Republic: Peale's Museum and Its Audience* (Washington, DC: Smithsonian Institution Press, 1995), 1.

6. Paul Finkelman, "Class and Culture in Late Nineteenth-Century Chicago: The Founding of the Newberry Library," *American Studies* 16 (1975): 6.

7. Helen Lefkowitz Horowitz, *Culture and the City: Cultural Philanthropy in Chicago from the 1880s to 1917* (Lexington: University Press of Kentucky, 1976), 29; Harold M. Mayer and Richard C. Wade, *Chicago: Growth of a Metropolis* (Chicago: University of Chicago Press, 1969), 35, 38.

8. Michael Kammen, *Mystic Chords of Memory: The Transformation of Tradition in American Culture* (New York: Vintage, 1991), 342.

9. Clement Silvestro, "The Candy Man's Mixed Bag," *Chicago History* 2 (Fall 1972): 89.

10. Walter Muir Whitehill, *Independent Historical Societies: An Enquiry into Their Research and Publications Functions and Their Financial Future* (Boston: Boston Athenaeum, distributed by Harvard University Press, 1962), 211–12.

11. CHS, *Annual Report, 1965–1966,* 15; Paul Angle quoted in Brubaker, "Urban History Research Center," 27.

12. John A. Williams, "American Historical Societies," in Charles Phillips and Patricia Hogan, eds., *Who Cares for America's Heritage?* (Nashville: American Association for State and Local History, 1984), 11.

13. Cynthia Jeffress Little, "Beyond Text Panels and Labels: Education and Public Programming in American Historical Societies," *Pennsylvania Magazine of History and Biography* 114 (January 1990): 88–89.

14. Matthew Gurewitsch, "The Brooklyn Museum Reaches Out—Again," *Wall Street Journal,* 15 April 2004, D6; Thomas P. F. Hoving, "Branch Out!" *Museum News* 46 (September 1968): 15.

15. Michael Kimmelman, "Culture and Race: Still on America's Mind," *New York Times,* 9 November 1995, B2(N); Allon Schoener, ed., *Harlem on My Mind: Cultural Capital of Black America, 1900–1968* (New York: Metropolitan Museum of Art, 1995), 14 (quotation).

16. Harold Skramstad, interview by author, tape recording, Henry Ford Museum, Dearborn, Michigan, May 13, 1996.

17. Marcia Froelke Coburn, "Dressed to Kill," *Chicago Magazine* (November 1992): 107.

18. Brubaker, "Urban History Research Center," 26.

19. Quoted in Richard Rabinowitz and Sam Bass Warner Jr., "Directions for American Historical Societies," *Chicago History* 10 (Fall 1981): 180.

20. David Kahn, "City History Museums as Social Instruments," paper presented at conference entitled "Venues of Inquiry into the American City: The Place of Museums, Libraries and Archives," CHS, October 29–30, 1990, 1.

21. Skramstad interview.

22. On September 16, 1970, CHS trustees reversed their long-standing policy of free admission and began charging a fifty-cent fee for adult visitors.

23. Joseph Zwyicki, "Painting and Sculpture Scope Statement," n.d. (Janice McNeill's personal files).

24. "Americans with Disabilities Act," *Museum News* 69 (January/February 1990): 26.

25. Carole Krucoff, "Renovating the Society's Fort Dearborn Exhibit," *Chicago History* 9 (Summer 1980): 119.

26. CHS, "Review of the Chicago Historical Society's Scope," n.d. (Janice McNeill's personal files).

27. "Questions for Scope Consultants," n.d. (Janice McNeill's personal files).

28. Letter from Thomas Schlereth to Ellsworth Brown, August 1, 1983 (Janice McNeill's personal files); Nicholas Westbrook, "Report to the Chicago Historical Society on Scope of Collections Study," August 1983 (Janice McNeill's personal files), 4, 8 (quotation).

29. CHS, "Collecting Policy," April 18, 1984 (Janice McNeill's personal files), reprinted in CHS, *Annual Report, 1983–1984,* 10.

30. Marc Hilton, interview by author, tape recording, Campbell and Company, Chicago, November 4, 1996.

31. CHS, *Annual Reports, 1984–1985,* 2, and *1988–1989,* 2.

32. For a detailed discussion of the growth of the design field see Larry Klein, "Team Players," *Museum News* 70 (March/April 1991): 44–45.

33. Amina Dickerson, Gayle Edmunds, and Lynn McRainey, interview by author, tape recording, CHS, November 22, 1996.

34. CHS, *Annual Report, 1987–1988,* 6 (quotation); CHS, "A Proposal to the Joyce Foundation in Support of the Chicago Historical Society's *Neighborhood: Keepers of Culture* Project," April 1992 (Russell Lewis's personal files), 1.

35. CHS, *Past Times* (September/October/November 1996), 2; CHS, *Annual Report, 1995–1996,* 6.

36. CHS, "Affirmative Action Task Force: Final Report and Recommendations," June 30, 1995 (Russell Lewis's personal files), 1.

37. CHS, *Annual Report, 1993–1994,* 5.

38. CHS, "The CHS Mission: Implications for the Future," *Strategic Plan* (1995), 6.

39. Stephanie Williams, "Giving a Voice to the Anonymous," *Chicago Reporter,* July 2001, http://www.findarticles.com/cf_dls/m0JAS/6_30/79250842/p1/articles.jhtml. Accessed February 17, 2004.

40. CHS, *Past Times* (March/April/May 2001), 3.

41. Lonnie Bunch, telephone interview by author, September 24, 2002.

42. Russell Lewis, telephone interview by author, April 7, 2004.

2: THE FIRST ACT

1. CHS, "*We the People* Opening Day Update," news release, August 28, 1987 (Alfred Young's personal files).

2. Susan G. Davis, "'Set Your Mood to Patriotic': History as Televised Special Event," *Radical History Review* 42 (September 1988): 127.

3. Commission on the Bicentennial of the U.S. Constitution, *A Guide to Celebrating the Bicentennial of the U.S. Constitution* (Washington, DC: Commission on the Bicentennial of the U.S. Constitution, June 1986), 8–9.

4. Ibid., 14–15.

5. David Kyvig, "The Constitution at 200: Historicism or Useful Public History?" *Public Historian* 10 (Winter 1988): 55. Kyvig explains, "In recommending Bowen to anyone who wants to know about the creation of the oldest existing national constitution, and who enjoys the excitement of world-historic drama told by a master storyteller . . . , Burger reveals something of his own view of history as static and unrelated to current policy issues" (59).

6. Michael Kammen, *A Machine that Would Go of Itself: The Constitution in American Culture* (New York: Alfred A. Knopf, 1986), 142 (1887); 283, 308 (Bloom).

7. Project '87, "The Bicentennial of the Constitution: A Look Ahead," *This Constitution* (September 1983): 36; Davis, "'Set Your Mood,'" 128.

8. Warren Leon, "Some Thoughts on Museums and the Constitution," *Museum News* 66 (August 1987): 25–26.

9. These exhibitions did not explore what historian Alice Kessler-Harris calls "the dynamic interaction of a multiracial and multiethnic population in an effort to understand how interest groups and classes compete for power and to develop a sense of how race, sex, and ethnicity mold and inhibit conceptions of common national purpose." See her essay "Social History," in Eric Foner, ed., *The New American History* (Philadelphia: Temple University Press, 1990), 233–34.

10. This is not to be confused with *The American Experiment: Creating the Constitution,* a yearlong exhibition at the National Archives that traced the new nation's development from the convening of the First Continental Congress through the adoption of the Constitution.

11. Leon, "Thoughts," 26.

12. Label copy, *Creating a New Nation, 1763–1803,* in the folder Exhibitions: *We the People,* Terry Fife 1, Creating a New Nation, CHS Archives.

13. Mary Janzen, "The Grant Process as a Tool for Exhibition Development—'We the People,' an NEH Success Story," paper presented at the American Association of Museums annual meeting, 1988, 1.

14. Terry Fife, interview by author, tape recording, Oak Park, Illinois, January 12, 1996.

15. Joseph Brown, "Celebrating the Ordinary in the Extraordinary," *Humanities Magazine* (September–October 1987): 32–33.

16. In *A Machine that Would Go of Itself,* Kammen argues that lamentations over public ignorance of the Constitution go in cycles, often skipping one generation. See chapters "God Knows How Dearly We Need a Constitutional Revival," 219–54, and "Our Bill of Rights Is under Subtle and Pervasive Attack," 336–56.

17. Mary Ellen Munley, "Evaluation Study Report: Visitors' Views of the 18th Century," paper presented at the Department of Social and Cultural History, National Museum of American History, July 1983, 37; Commission on the Bicentennial of the U.S. Constitution, *Guide,* 3. For the Hearst Corporation see Tom Gibbons, "Americans' Knowledge of Constitution Slim," *Chicago Sun-Times,* 16 March 1987, 6. The Center for Judicial Studies published a report that echoed these findings. See *Democracy at Risk: The Rising Tide of Political Illiteracy and Ignorance of the Constitution* (Washington, DC: Center for Judicial Studies, 1984), cited in Kammen, *Machine,* 383.

18. Kammen, *Machine,* 374.

19. James W. Loewen, *Lies My Teacher Told Me: Everything Your American History Textbook Got Wrong* (New York: New Press, 1995), 358. See Robert M. O'Neil, "The Constitution, the Supreme Court, and Youth," *Social Education* 37 (1973): 397–99, cited in Kammen, *Machine,* 385.

20. The first schoolbook to discuss the Constitution was *A Plain Political Catechism,* published in 1796. Kammen, *Machine,* 14.

21. Kammen, *Machine,* 14. These kinds of pressures lead to the blatant inaccuracies that Michael Kammen chronicles in his chapter "The Problems of Constitutionalism in American Culture," in *Machine,* 3–39.

22. These criteria are drawn from a list of recommendations proposed by two scholars of social studies education, Shirley Engle and Anna Ochoa, in 1986 (see Loewen, *Lies,* 266).

23. Other revisionist texts include Mary Beth Norton et al., *A People and a Nation: A History of the United States* (Boston: Houghton Mifflin, 1982); Gary B. Nash et al., *The American People: Creating a Nation and a Society* (New York: Collins College, 1986); James A. Henretta et al., *America's History* (Chicago: Dorsey Press, 1987); Edward Countryman, Marcus Rediker, et al., *Who Built America?* (New York: American Social History Project, 1990).

24. Leon, "Thoughts," 26.

25. For a discussion of these stages and the historians who helped shape them, see Kessler-Harris, "Social History," 231–55; Alfred F. Young, "Introduction," in *Beyond the American Revolution: Explorations in the History of American Radicalism,* ed. Alfred F. Young (DeKalb: Northern Illinois University Press, 1983), 5; Edmund S. Morgan, *The Birth of the Republic, 1763–1789* (Chicago: University of Chicago Press, 1956); Bernard Bailyn, *The Ideological Origins of the American Revolution* (Cambridge: Belknap Press of Harvard University Press, 1967); Benjamin Wright, *Consensus and Continuity, 1776–1787* (Boston: Boston University Press, 1958).

26. Alfred Young, ed. *Dissent: Explorations in the History of American Radicalism* (DeKalb: Northern Illinois University Press, 1968); Young, *Beyond the American Revolution,* 7; Jesse Lemisch, "The Radicalism of the Inarticulate: Merchant Seamen in the Politics of Revolutionary America," in Young, *Dissent,* 37–82.

27. Alfred Young, ed. *The American Revolution: Explorations in the History of American Radicalism* (DeKalb: Northern Illinois University Press, 1976), 8; Gary B. Nash, *The Urban Crucible: Social Change, Political Consciousness, and the Origins of the American Revolution* (Cambridge, MA: Harvard University Press, 1979); Edward Countryman, *A People in Revolution: The American Revolution and the Political Society in New York, 1760–1790* (Baltimore: Johns Hopkins University Press, 1981); Eric Foner, *Tom Paine and Revolutionary America* (New York: Oxford University Press, 1976).

28. Young, *Beyond the American Revolution,* 3.

29. Alfred Young, interview by author, tape recording, Oak Park, Illinois, January 11, 1996. Young mentioned the following titles: Herbert Aptheker, *The Negro in the American Revolution* (New York: International Publishers, 1940); Benjamin Quarles, *The Negro in the American Revolution* (Chapel Hill: University of North Carolina Press, 1961); Eugene Genovese, *Roll, Jordan, Roll: The World the Slaves Made* (New York: Vintage Books, 1974); Herbert Gutman, *The Black Family in Slavery and Freedom, 1750–1925* (New York: Pantheon Books, 1976); Ira Berlin, *Slaves without Masters: The Free Negro in the Antebellum South* (New York: Pantheon, 1974); Roger Butterfield, *The American Past: A History of the U.S. from Concord to Hiroshima, 1775–1945* (New York: Simon and Schuster, 1947); Sidney Kaplan, *The Black Presence in the Era of the American Revolution, 1770–1800* (Greenwich, CT: New York Graphic Society, 1973); Linda DePauw and Conover Hunt, *Remember the Ladies: Women in America, 1750–1815* (New York: Viking Press, 1976); Barbara Graymont, *The Iroquois in the American Revolution* (Syracuse, NY: Syracuse University Press, 1972); Wilcomb Washburn, *The Indian in America* (New York: Harper and Row, 1975); Gary B. Nash, *Red, White, and Black: The People of Early America* (Englewood Cliffs, NJ: Prentice Hall, 1991); and Helen Tanner, *Atlas of Great Lakes Indian History* (Norman: Oklahoma University Press, 1987).

30. For a full discussion of this point, see Carol Duncan, "Art Museums and the Rituals of Citizenship," in Karp and Lavine, *Exhibiting Cultures,* 90–91.

31. Edward Linenthal discusses this dilemma in *Sacred Ground: Americans and Their Battlefields* (Urbana: University of Illinois Press, 1991), 4–5, arguing that commemorations and anniversaries serve as opportunities for the public to remember and

reaffirm the ideals of cultural heroes. Although writing about American attitudes toward battlefields, his discussion is useful here because it explains why revisionist scholarship might be considered heretical in museums.

32. Alfred F. Young, "'Ordinary People' in Great Events: An American Museum Experience, Chicago Historical Society," *History Workshop* 32 (Autumn 1991): 212.

33. These distinctions are based on a detailed discussion by Fath Davis Ruffins in "An Elegant Metaphor," *Museum News* 64 (October 1985): 56, 58–59.

34. Claudine Brown, quoted in Donald Garfield, "Hard Money: Funders Talk about Funding for Museums," *Museum News* 74 (September/October 1995): 62.

3: WE THE PEOPLE AS AN AGENT OF CHANGE

1. Mary Janzen, interview by author, tape recording, CHS, January 26, 1996; Letter from Richard Leffler to Mary Janzen, January 18, 1984, in the folder Exhibitions: Education Criticism, *We the People,* 6, CHS Archives.

2. Mary Janzen, "Collaborative Risk-Taking: Making 'We the People' at the Chicago Historical Society," *Journal of American Culture* 12 (Summer 1989): 74.

3. Ibid.

4. Ibid., 73; Young interview.

5. Alfred Young and Terry Fife, interview by author, tape recording, CHS, January 19, 1996.

6. CHS, *Annual Report, 1986–1987,* 17.

7. Janzen, "Collaborative Risk-Taking," 72.

8. James William Miller, "Museums and the Academy: Toward Building an Alliance," *Journal of American Culture* 12 (Summer 1989): 1.

9. Young interview.

10. *We the People,* visitor survey, no. 5, January 6, 1996.

11. Leo Burnett Company, Inc., "Chicago Historical Society, Part I: Aware Non-Visitors, Visitors," June 1988, 13, and "Part II: New Members, Continuing Members, Lapsed Members," June 1988, 4; Metro Chicago Information Center (MCIC), chapter 4, "The Chicago Historical Society," in "Chicago Tourism Profile: A Report on Tourist Surveys Undertaken at Cultural and Non-Cultural Destinations in the Chicago Area," October 1995, 1–12.

12. Of the 102 survey respondents, 76 answered the question "What was the first exhibition you visited today?" and only 15 (19 percent) answered *We the People.*

13. Nancy Wilson, interview by author, tape recording, CHS, January 16, 1996.

14. John H. Falk and Lynn D. Dierking make this distinction in *The Museum Experience* (Washington, DC: Whalesback Books, 1992), 73. See also Stephen Bitgood and Donald Patterson, "The Effects of Gallery Changes on Visitor Reading and Object Viewing Time," *Environment and Behavior* 25 (November 1993): 761–81.

15. Armita Neal, *Exhibit Handbook for Small Museums* (Nashville: American Association of State and Local History, 1976), 122, 130.

16. Ellsworth Brown, e-mail correspondence with author, June 19, 1996. In "Effects of Gallery Changes," Bitgood and Patterson argue that the location of exhibition labels has a direct bearing on the visitors' willingness to read them.

17. Paul Apodaca, e-mail response to author's posting, "How Long Do Visitors Spend Reading Labels?" on the MUSEUM-L electronic bulletin board, June 11, 1996, accessible through LISTSERV@UNMVMA.UNM.EDU.

18. *We the People,* visitor survey, no. 70, January 20, 1996.

19. Young interview.

20. *We the People,* visitor survey, no. 13, January 7, 1996; Young interview.

21. Of 102 surveys collected, 37 visitors made some mention of these groups. This group spent an average of 44 minutes in the gallery, the same as the average visitor.

22. *We the People,* visitor surveys, no. 5, January 6; no. 25, January 8; nos. 38, 39, January 10; no. 59, January 16; nos. 67, 68, 69, 71, January 20; no. 87, January 27; all in 1996.

23. Ibid., no. 16, January 7; no. 22, January 8; both in 1996.

24. Fife interview.

25. Janzen, "Grant Process," 7.

26. Little, "Beyond Text Panels," 86.

27. CHS curator, interview by author, tape recording, CHS, January 10, 1996.

28. Ellsworth Brown, interview by author, tape recording, Pittsburgh, Pennsylvania, November 9, 1995.

29. Letter from Alfred Young to Marc Hilton, October 28, 1987 (Alfred Young's personal files).

30. See, all in *Museum News,* Dorothy A. Mariner, "Professionalizing the Museum Worker," 50 (June 1972): 14–20; Barrie Reynolds, "Are Curators Second-Class Citizens?" 52 (May 1974): 33–35; Bret Waller, "Museum Training: Who Needs It?" 52 (May 1974): 26–28; Kenneth Starr, "A Perspective on Our Profession," 58 (May/June 1980): 21–23; "Suggested Qualifications for Museum Positions," 59 (October 1980): 27–31; "Criteria for Examining Professional Museum Studies Programs," 62 (June 1983): 70–72.

31. Mariner, "Museum Worker," 14.

32. CHS curator, interview by author, tape recording, Chicago, Illinois, March 22, 1996; Russell Lewis, CHS, *Annual Report, 1986–1987,* 7.

33. Letter from Alfred Young to Ellsworth Brown, July 27, 1987 (Alfred Young's personal files).

34. *We the People,* visitor surveys, no. 5, January 6; no. 39, January 10; no. 48, January 13; all in 1996.

35. Ibid., no. 23, January 9; no. 35, January 10; both in 1996.

36. For a more detailed discussion of this issue, see Hal K. Rothman, "Museums and Academics: Thoughts toward an Ethic of Cooperation," *Journal of American Culture* 12 (Summer 1989): 35.

37. Alfred Young, Terry Fife, and Mary Janzen, *We the People: Voices and Images of the New Nation* (Philadelphia: Temple University Press, 1993), xxi.

38. Eric Foner, e-mail correspondence with author, June 17, 1996; Terry Fife, telephone interview by author, July 9, 1996.

39. Marsha Semmel, telephone interview by author, July 11, 1996.

40. Mary Janzen, Cynthia Little, Elizabeth Jarvis, telephone interviews by author, July 16, 17, 19, 1996, respectively.

41. Janzen telephone interview.

4: THE TRANSITION YEARS, 1987–1993

1. Edith P. Mayo, "Exhibiting Politics," *Museum News* (September/October 1992): 50.

2. Richard Armey quoted in Phillip Brookman, preface to Bolton, *Culture Wars,* xvi.

3. Kevin M. Guthrie, *The New-York Historical Society: Lessons from One Non-Profit's Long Struggle for Survival* (San Francisco: Jossey-Bass, 1996), 111–12.

4. CHS, "Request for a Grant from John D. and Catherine T. MacArthur Foundation," 6.

5. Nina Kressner Cobb, *Looking Ahead: Private Sector Giving to the Arts and Humanities* (Washington, DC: President's Commission on the Arts and Humanities, 1996), 10.

6. William Grimes, "Tough Line on Grants for Arts: Shape Up," *New York Times,* August 5, 1996, 7.

7. CHS, "Request for a Grant from John D. and Catherine T. MacArthur Foundation," 6.

8. Cherry Schroeder, "Diverse Audiences: How Do We Get 'Em into the Museum?" *Museum Education* (Getty Museum newsletter), n.d.

9. Emma Lapsansky, "City Museums as Sources," paper presented at conference entitled "Venues of Inquiry into the American City: The Place of Museums, Libraries and Archives," CHS, October 29-30, 1990, 3.

10. Robin Cembalest, "Goodbye, Columbus?" *ARTnews* 90 (October 1991): 105.

11. Jay Pridmore, "A Museum Comes of Age: Historical Society Tells City's Story," *Chicago Tribune,* February 22, 1991, CN3.

12. Susan Page Tillett, interview by author, tape recording, Chicago, Illinois, March 27, 1996.

13. Susan Page Tillett, "Staff Development: A Sound Investment," in Susan K. Nichols, ed., *Staff Development: Innovative Techniques* (Washington, DC: American Association of Museums, Technical Information Service, 1989), 29.

14. David Garfield, "Inspiring Change: Post-Heroic Management, an Interview with Harold Skramstad and Steve Hamp at the Henry Ford Museum," *Museum News* (January/February 1995): 47.

15. Harold K. Skramstad, "Introduction," in Nichols, *Staff Development,* ii.

16. Handout, "Heroic Leadership and Post-Heroic Leadership," Museum Management Institute's Curriculum Materials, 1992 (Amina Dickerson's personal files).

17. Allan R. Cohen and David L. Bradford, "Influence without Authority: The Use of Alliances, Reciprocity, and Exchange to Accomplish Work," *Organizational Dynamics* 17 (Winter 1989): 7.

18. Janes, *Museums,* 158, 43.

19. Sharon Darling, Carole Krucoff, Mary Janzen, Wim de Wit, "Report of the Staff Exhibitions Committee," CHS, July 8, 1985 (Russell Lewis's personal files), 14-15.

20. Gaynor Kavanagh discusses this issue in *History Curatorship* (Washington, DC: Smithsonian Press, 1990), 119-20.

21. CHS, *Annual Report, 1989-1990.*

22. Detroit Historical Department and Detroit Historical Society, "Mission Statements of the Detroit Historical Department and Detroit Historical Society," 1989 (Amina Dickerson's personal files).

23. Barbara Franco, "Personal Connections to History: The Context for a Changing Historical Society," *Washington History* (Fall/Winter 1995-1996): 29.

24. CHS, Collections and Exhibitions Committee, "Mission Statement Recommended to the Board of Trustees," March 11, 1989 (Robert Nauert's personal files), 4.

25. David Kahn elaborates on the issue of naming the institution in "City Museums as Social Instruments," paper presented at the conference entitled "Venues of Inquiry in the American City: The Place of Museums, Libraries, and Archives," CHS, October 29-30, 19.

26. CHS, *Past Times* (March/April 1992), 3.

27. Kahn, "City History Museums," 1, 5.

28. Amina J. Dickerson, "Modes to What End? Scholarship, Museums and Community Transformation," paper presented at conference entitled "Venues of Inquiry into the American City: The Place of Museums, Libraries, and Archives," CHS, October 29–30, 1990, 21–22.

29. Russell Lewis, interview by author, tape recording, CHS, November 8, 1996.

30. CHS, "Illinois Humanities Council Grant Application," March 14, 1990, 7.

31. Amina J. Dickerson, "Modes to What End?" 3.

32. Blake McKelvey, "Legacy," *Urban History Newsletter* 1 (March 1989): 4.

33. This brief history of the field is primarily drawn from Michael Ebner's article, "Urban History: Retrospect and Prospect," *Journal of American History* 68 (June 1981): 69–84.

34. Stephan Thernstrom and Richard Sennett, eds., *Nineteenth-Century Cities: Essays in the New Urban History* (New Haven: Yale University Press, 1969), quoted in Ebner, "Urban History," 74.

35. This brief history of the UHA and CHS Urban History Seminar is based on two interviews: Michael Ebner, telephone interview by author, December 16, 1996, and Robert Goler, interview by author, tape recording, S. Dillon Ripley Center, Washington, DC, July 2, 1996.

36. Laura Chapman, "The Future of Museum Education," *Museum News* (July/August 1992): 53.

37. See John Cotton Dana, *The New Museum* (Woodstock, VT: Elm Tree Press, 1917) and *A Plan for a New Museum* (Woodstock, VT: Elm Tree Press, 1920); Benjamin Ives Gilman, *Museum Ideals of Purpose and Method* (Cambridge, MA: Riverside Press, 1918); Henry Watson Kent, ed., *What I Am Pleased to Call My Education* (New York: Grolier Club, 1949).

38. CHS, "Request for a Grant from John D. and Catherine T. MacArthur Foundation," 5–6.

39. Dickerson, Edmunds, and McRainey interview.

40. American Association of Museums, *Museums for a New Century: A Report of the Commission on Museums for a New Century* (Washington, DC: AAM, 1984), 63.

41. Berger discusses this problem in "Are Art Museums Racist?" 70.

5: THE *NEIGHBORHOODS* PROJECT

1. AAM, *Museums for a New Century,* 75.

2. Thomas L. Haskell, ed., *The Authority of Experts: Studies in History and Theory* (Bloomington: Indiana University Press, 1984), xv. See also Louis Menand, "The Trashing of Professionalism," *New York Times Magazine,* 5 March 1995; and Franco, "Doing History," 5.

3. Otis L. Graham, "Who Owns History?" *Public Historian* 17 (Spring 1995): 8.

4. Brown, "Keynote Address," in Tolles, *Museum Curatorship,* 17.

5. NEH, "How the Endowment Works," *Eighteenth Annual Report (1983),* 11–12, and "The Purpose of Challenge Grants," *Seventeenth Annual Report (1982),* 18.

6. For a more complete listing of these efforts, see American Association of Museums, *Museums: Their New Audiences* (Washington, DC: AAM, 1972), and Mike Wallace, "Razor Ribbons, History Museums, Civic Salvation," in *Mickey Mouse History,* 34–54.

7. Joyce Foundation, "1992 Request for Proposals," May 28, 1992 (CHS development office files).

8. Patricia Mooney-Melvin, interview with author, tape recording, Chicago, November 5, 1996.

9. Susan Samek, interview by author, tape recording, CHS, April 2, 1996.

10. CHS curator, interview by author, tape recording, CHS, January 22, 1996.

11. Barbara Franco makes this argument in her discussion of a similar initiative at the Minnesota Historical Society. See "Doing History," 7.

12. Community partner, follow-up meeting in Rogers Park, tape recording, Chicago, January 17, 1996.

13. CHS, "Rogers Park/West Ridge: Historical Timeline," press packet 1996, 4.

14. *Rogers Park/West Ridge,* visitor surveys, no. 3, January 5; no. 47, January 10; no. 67, January 14; no. 105, January 19; no. 146, March 31; all in 1996.

15. Timuel Black, interview by author, tape recording, DuSable Museum, Chicago, March 28, 1996; Mikel Brissee, follow-up meeting in Rogers Park, tape recording, Chicago, January 17, 1996.

16. Tracye Matthews, interview by author, tape recording, CHS, January 9, 1996.

17. Community partner, follow-up meeting in Rogers Park, tape recording, Chicago, January 17, 1996.

18. Black interview.

19. Olivia Mahoney, e-mail correspondence to author, February 24, 1997.

20. *Rogers Park/West Ridge,* visitor surveys, no. 78, January 14; no. 19, January 7; both in 1996.

21. Gerda Lerner makes these important distinctions in "Placing Women in History: Definitions and Challenges," in *The Majority Finds Its Past* (New York: Oxford University Press, 1979), 145–59.

22. Wallace makes a similar argument in "Museums and Controversy," in *Mickey Mouse History,* 34–54.

23. Franco, "Doing History," 8.

24. Olivia Mahoney, interview by author, tape recording, CHS, January 22, 1996.

25. Theodore Berland, "History Distorted," *Chicago Tribune,* 16 December 1995, 22.

26. Both Burroughs and Tortolero from Charles Storch, "Museums in an Ethnic Turf Battle," *Chicago Tribune,* 14 September 1994, N1.

27. CHS, "Rogers Park Comments," January–March 1996 (Russell Lewis's personal files).

28. Tracye Matthews, interview by author, tape recording, CHS, January 17, 1996.

29. June Finfer, follow-up meeting in Rogers Park, tape recording, Chicago, January 17, 1996.

30. Douglas Greenberg, e-mail correspondence with author, March 18, 1997.

31. Ellsworth Brown to Alfred Young, August 13, 1987 (Alfred Young's personal files).

32. Russell Lewis, telephone interview by author, September 14, 2002.

33. Mahoney interview.

34. CHS, "Rogers Park/West Ridge: Rhythms of Diversity," *Gallery Guide,* 1995, 2, in Russell Lewis's personal files.

35. John Russick, telephone interview with author, September 25, 2002.

36. Wallace, *Mickey Mouse History,* 43.

37. Cary Carson, "City Museums as Historians," paper presented at conference entitled "Venues of Inquiry into the American City: The Place of Museums, Libraries, and Archives," CHS, October 29–30, 1990, 30.

38. Mooney-Melvin interview.

39. Cheryl L. Kennedy, "Collaborative Projects," response to author's posting on MUSEUM-L e-mail bulletin board, January 13, 1996, accessible through LISTSERVE@UNMVMA.UNM.EDU.

6: UNFINISHED BUSINESS

1. Nicholas Westbrook, "Report to the Chicago Historical Society on Scope of Collections Study," August 1983 (Janice McNeill's personal files), 12.

2. Franco, "Doing History," 6.

3. CHS, "The Chicago Historical Society Today: Strengths and Challenges," *Strategic Plan (1995)*, 5, in Russell Lewis's personal files; Phyllis Rabineau, e-mail correspondence to author, November 19, 2002; Andrew Herrmann, "Attendance down Last Year at More than Half of the City's Biggest Museums," *Chicago Sun Times*, 29 January 2004, 3.

4. This discussion is based on David A. Aaker, *Strategic Market Management* (New York: John Wiley & Sons, 1992).

5. Pierre Bourdieu and Alain Darbel, *The Love of Art: European Museums and Their Public* (Stanford: Stanford University Press, 1990), 14.

6. Pamela Mays McDonald, "The Bay Area Research Project: A Review through the Dark Eyes of One Hundred Years Ago," paper presented at conference entitled "Audience Development: Marketing for Diverse Audiences," at the Graduate Department of Museum Studies, John F. Kennedy University, n.d., 14. She bases much of her argument on J. Mark David Schuster's *The Audience for American Art Museums* (Washington, DC: Seven Locks Press, 1992).

7. For a more detailed discussion of the broadening of the conception of difference, see Claudine K. Brown, "The Museum's Role in a Multicultural Society," in Museum Education Roundtable, *Patterns in Practice: Selections from the Journal of Museum Education* (Washington, DC: Museum Educational Roundtable, 1992): 3–8. Bourdieu and Darbel argue that museums must challenge "the untouchability of objects, the religious silence which imposes itself on visitors, the puritan asceticism of the amenities, always sparse and rather uncomfortable, the quasi-systematic absence of any information, [and] the grandiose solemnity of decor and decorum." *Love of Art*, 112.

8. Kathryn Mathers, *Museums, Galleries and New Audiences* (London: Art and Society, 1996), 9.

9. Rob Parel, "Chicago's Immigrants Break Old Patterns," Migration Information Source, at http://www.migrationinformation/org/USfocus/display.cfm?ID=160.

10. Paula Terry, "New Roles Will Require Even Greater Access to Museums," *Museum News* (January/February 1990): 26.

11. CHS staff member, interview by author, tape recording, Chicago, March 27, 1996.

12. See Thomas Schlereth, "Causing Conflict, Doing Violence," *Museum News* (October 1984): 46.

13. CHS board minutes, 9 February 1994 (General Administration, Trustee Minutes, CHS Archives), 13.

14. See Alfred Young, "A Modest Proposal: A Bill of Rights for American Museums," *Public Historian* 14 (Summer 1992): 67–75.

15. Steven C. Dubin examines this issue in *Displays of Power: Controversy in the American Museum from the Enola Gay to Sensation* (New York: New York University Press, 1999), 3.

16. Duncan, "Art Museums," 92.

17. Ibid., 90–91.

18. Pamela Newkirk, "Searching for the Black Audience," *ArtNews* (May 2001): 187.

19. See Charles Phillips and Patricia Hogan, *The Wages of History: The AASLH Employment Trends and Salary Survey* (Nashville: American Association for State and Local History, 1984), 29; Marcia Tucker, "Common Ground," *Museum News* 69 (July/August 1990): 44–46.

20. American Association of Museums, *Museums: Their New Audience*, 10.

EPILOGUE

1. "Other Exhibits in Chicago," *State Journal-Register* (Springfield, IL) 9 November 2003, 27.

2. Angle, "Chicago Historical Society," 58.

3. Williams, "Voice to the Anonymous," n.p.

4. CHS, *Past Times* (March/April/May 2001), 2.

5. David Ebony, "Museum Attendance on the Rise," *Art in America* 1.87 (March 1999): 27; "And Still the Crowds Come," *Economist*, 5 March 2001, 77; Judith H. Dobrzynski, "Blockbuster Shows Lure Record Crowds into U.S. Museums," *New York Times*, 3 February 2000, E5.

6. "Comment: Museum Attendance," *Wall Street Journal*, 16 February 2000, A24.

7. Judith Dobrzynski, "Art Museum Attendance Keeps Rising in U.S." *New York Times*, 1 February 1999, E1.

8. Dobrzynski, "Blockbuster Shows," E5.

9. "Museums: Firsts, Facts and Figures," *New York Times*, 19 April 2000, 20.

10. American Association of Museums, "Museum and Community Initiative," http://www.aam-us/org/initiatives/m&c/index.cfm. Accessed September 6, 2002.

11. Kinshasha Holman Conwill and Alexandra Marmion Roosa, "Cultivating Community Connections," *Museum News* (May/June 2003): 42.

12. Lonnie G. Bunch, "In the Shadow of Uncertainty: Museums in the Aftermath," *Museum News* (January/February 2002): 41.

13. Margo Bloom, Edward T. Linenthal, and Kym S. Rice, "Museums and Communities after September 11," *Journal of American History* 89.3 (December 2002): 1014–16; Robert McDonald, "9/11: The World Transformed," *Museum News* (November/December 2001): 36.

14. "Community Gathering: A Report from the Field," *Museum News* (November/December 2001): 37.

15. Bloom, Linenthal, and Rice, "Museums and Communities," 1016. The Chester County Historical Society's program was divided into three parts: "Understanding Islam" on November 27, 2001, "The Responsibility of the Press" on December 4, 2001, and "Democratic Institutions and Civil Liberties in a Time of National Crisis" on December 11, 2001.

16. Bunch, "Shadow of Uncertainty," 41.

17. CHS, *Past Times* (September/October/November 2002), 3.

18. Bunch, "Shadow of Uncertainty," 41.

19. Ibid., 39.

20. Robin Pogrebin, "New York Arts Being Cut Back in Money Pinch," *New York Times*, 11 February 2003, A1; Frank Shafroth, "Deep Cuts: The Crisis in State Funding," *Museum News* (July/August 2003): 30–33; Bourscheidt quoted from Pogrebin, "Arts Being Cut Back," A1; attendance percentages from Bunch, "Shadow of Uncertainty," 39.

21. Brian McCormick, "Gallery of Competition," *Crain's Chicago Business,* 29 September 2003, 4.

22. Russell Lewis, telephone interview by author, April 7, 2004.

23. Klaus Mueller, "Invisible Visitors: Museums and the Gay and Lesbian Community," *Museum News* (September/October 2001): 34–39, 67, 69.

24. Paulette V. Maehara, "Seeing the Forest: The New Donor Demographics," *Museum News* (September/October 2003): 33.

25 Paulette V. Maehara, "Giving in America: Six New Trends in Fundraising," *Museum News* (March/April 2003): 62.

26. Michael Wolfe and Robert Ferguson, "New Money, New Demands: The Arrival of the Venture Philanthropist," *Museum News* (January/February 2001): 56.

27. Lonnie Bunch, "Challenges of Diversity," http://www.joycefdn.org/programs/culture/content/zspots/lonniebunch.html Accessed February 17, 2004.

28. David M. Darlington, "Facing 'The Perfect Storm,'" *Museum News* (July/August 2003): 35.

29. Herlinda Zamora, "Identity and Community: A Look at Four Latino Museums," *Museum News* (May/June 2002): 37.

30. Randi Korn, "Self-Portrait: First Know Thyself, Then Serve Your Public," *Museum News* (January/February 2004): 33–35, 50–52 (35).

Works Cited

Aaker, David A. *Strategic Market Management*. New York: John Wiley & Sons, 1992.

Adams, Robert McCormack. "Smithsonian Horizons." *Smithsonian* 23 (April 1992): 13–14.

American Association of Museums. *Mastering Civic Engagement: A Challenge to Museums*. Washington, D.C.: American Association of Museums, 2002.

——. "Museum and Community Initiative." http://www.aam-us/org/initiatives/m&c/index.cfm. Accessed September 6, 2002.

——. *Museums for a New Century: A Report of the Commission on Museums for a New Century*. Washington, D.C.: American Association of Museum, 1984.

——. *Museums: Their New Audience*. Washington, D.C.: American Association of Museums, 1972.

——. *Staff Development: Innovative Techniques*. Washington, D.C.: American Association of Museums, Technical Information Service, 1989.

"Americans with Disabilities Act." *Museum News* (January/February 1990): 26.

"And Still the Crowds Come." *Economist*, 3 March 2001, 77.

Angle, Paul. "The Chicago Historical Society, 1856–1946." *Chicago History* 1 (Fall 1945–Summer 1948): 57–85.

Aptheker, Herbert. *The Negro in the American Revolution*. New York: International Publishers, 1940.

Archibald, Robert. *A Place to Remember: Using History to Build Community*. Walnut Creek, CA: AltaMira Press, 1999.

Arts Wire Current. http://www.artswire.org/current/1999/cur100599.html. Accessed October 5, 1999.

Bailyn, Bernard. *The Ideological Origins of the American Revolution*. Cambridge: Belknap Press of Harvard University Press, 1967.

Benson, Susan Porter, Stephen Brier, and Roy Rosenzweig, eds. *Presenting the Past: Essays on History and the Public*. Philadelphia: Temple University Press, 1986.

Berger, Maurice. "Are Art Museums Racist?" *Art in America* 68 (September 1990): 69–76.

Berland, Thedore. "History Distorted." *Chicago Tribune*, 16 December 1995, 22.

Berlin, Ira. *Slaves without Masters: The Free Negro in the Antebellum South*. New York: Pantheon, 1974.

Bitgood, Stephen, and Donald Patterson. "The Effects of Gallery Changes on Visitor Reading and Object Viewing Time." *Environment and Behavior* 25 (November 1993): 761–81.

Blackmon, Carolyn P., Teresa K. LaMaster, Lisa C. Roberts, and Beverly Serrell. *Open Conversations: Strategies for Professional Development in Museums.* Chicago: Department of Education, Field Museum of Natural History, 1988.

Bloom, Margo, Edward T. Linenthal, and Kym S. Rice. "Museums and Communities after September 11." *Journal of American History* 89.3 (December 2002): 1014–16.

Bolton, Richard, ed. *Culture Wars: Documents from Recent Controversies in the Arts.* New York: New Press, 1992.

Bourdieu, Pierre, and Alain Darbel. *The Love of Art: European Museums and Their Public.* Stanford: Stanford University Press, 1990.

Brigham, David R. *Public Culture in the Early Republic: Peale's Museum and Its Audience.* Washington, D.C.: Smithsonian Institution Press, 1995.

Brown, Ellsworth. "The Society: Preserving and Interpreting the Past." *Chicago History* (Fall 1981): 190–91.

Brown, Joseph. "Celebrating the Ordinary in the Extraordinary." *Humanities Magazine* (September-October 1987): 32–33.

Brubaker, Robert L. "The Development of an Urban History Research Center: The Chicago Historical Society's Library." *Chicago History* 7 (Spring 1978): 22–36.

Bunch, Lonnie G. "Challenges of Diversity." http://www.joycefdn.org/programs/culture/content/zspots/lonniebunch.htmlAccessed February 17, 2004.

———. "In the Shadow of Uncertainty: Museums in the Aftermath." *Museum News* (January/February 2002): 39–41.

Butterfield, Roger. *The American Past: A History of the U.S. from Concord to Hiroshima, 1775–1945.* New York: Simon and Schuster, 1947.

Byrk, Nancy Villa. "Reports of Our Death Have Been Greatly Exaggerated: Reconsidering the Curator." *Museum News* (March/April 2001): 39–41, 67–71.

Cameron, Duncan. "The Museum: A Temple or the Forum." *Journal of World History* 14.1 (1972): 197–210.

Carson, Cary. "City Museums as Historians." Paper presented at Venues of Inquiry into the American City: The Place of Museums, Libraries, and Archives. Chicago Historical Society, October 29–30, 1990.

Cembalest, Robin. "Goodbye, Columbus?" *ARTnews* 90 (October 1991): 104–9.

Center for Judicial Studies. *Democracy at Risk: The Rising Tide of Political Illiteracy and Ignorance of the Constitution.* Washington, D.C.: Center for Judicial Studies, 1984.

Chapman, Laura. "The Future and Museum Education." *Museum News* (July/August 1992): 48–55.

Chicago Historical Society. *Annual Reports,* 1936–2003.

———. Exhibitions, Chicago Historical Society Archives.

———. General Administration, Chicago Historical Society Archives.

———. *Past Times,* 1986–2004.

———. "Request for a Grant from John D. and Catherine T. MacArthur Foundation." February 1, 1993. Robert Nauert's personal files.

Cobb, Nina Kressner. *Looking Ahead: Private Sector Giving to the Arts and Humanities.* Washington, D.C.: President's Commission on the Arts and Humanities, 1996.

Coburn, Marcia Froelke. "Dressed to Kill." *Chicago Magazine* (November 1992): 104–7, 146–52.

Cohen, Allan R., and David L. Bradford. "Influence without Authority: The Use of Alliances, Reciprocity, and Exchange to Accomplish Work," *Organizational Dynamics* 17 (Winter 1989): 5–17.

"Comment: Museum Attendance." *Wall Street Journal,* 16 February 2000, A24.

Commission on the Bicentennial of the United States Constitution. *A Guide to Celebrating the Bicentennial of the U.S. Constitution.* Washington: Commission on the Bicentennial of the United States Constitution, June 1986.

"Community Gathering: A Report from the Field." *Museum News* (November/December 2001): 37, 62–65.

Conwill, Kinshasha Holman, and Alexandra Marmion Roosa, "Cultivating Community Connections." *Museum News* (May/June 2003): 41–47.

Countryman, Edward. *A People in Revolution: The American Revolution and the Political Society in New York, 1760–1790.* Baltimore: Johns Hopkins University Press, 1981.

Countryman, Edward, Marcus Rediker, et al. *Who Built America?* New York: American Social History Project, 1990.

"Criteria for Examining Professional Museum Studies Programs." *Museum News* 62 (June 1983): 70–72.

Dana, John Cotton. *The New Museum.* Woodstock, VT: Elm Tree Press, 1917.

———. *A Plan for a New Museum.* Woodstock, VT: Elm Tree Press, 1920.

Darlington, David M. "Facing 'The Perfect Storm'." *Museum News* (July/August 2003): 33–35.

Davis, Susan G. "'Set Your Mood to Patriotic': History as Televised Special Event." *Radical History Review* 42 (September 1988): 122–43.

Davis, Thomas J. "They Too Were Here: The Afro-American Experience and History Museums." *American Quarterly* 41 (June 1989): 328–40.

Dennis, Emily. "Seminar on Neighborhood Museums." *Museum News* 48 (January 1970): 13–19.

DePauw, Linda, and Conover Hunt. *Remember the Ladies: Women in America, 1750–1815.* New York: Viking Press, 1976.

Dickerson, Amina. "Modes to What End? Scholarship, Museums and Community Transformation." Paper presented at "Venues of Inquiry into the American City: The Place of Museums, Libraries, and Archives." Session 3. Chicago Historical Society, October 29–30, 1990.

Dobrzynski, Judith H. "Art Museum Attendance Keeps Rising in U.S." *New York Times,* 1 February 1999, E1, E3.

———. "Blockbuster Shows Lure Record Crowds into U.S. Museums." *New York Times,* 3 February 2000, E5.

Dubin, Steven C. *Displays of Power: Controversy in the American Museum from the Enola Gay to Sensation.* New York: New York University Press, 1999.

Duncan, Carol. "Art Museums and the Rituals of Citizenship." In *Exhibiting Cultures: The Poetics and Politics of Museum Display,* ed. Ivan Karp and Steven Lavine, 88–103. Washington, D.C.: Smithsonian Institution Press, 1991.

Ebner, Michael. "Urban History: Retrospect and Prospect." *Journal of American History* 68 (June 1981): 69–84.

Ebony, David. "Museum Attendance on the Rise." *Art in America* 1.87 (March 1999): 27.

Falk, John H., and Lynn D. Dierking. *The Museum Experience.* Washington, D.C.: Whalesback Books, 1992.

Finkelman, Paul. "Class and Culture in Late Nineteenth-Century Chicago: The Founding of the Newberry Library." *American Studies* 16 (1975): 5–22.

Fisher, Marc. "Under Attack, Library Shelves Freud Exhibit," *Washington Post,* December 1, 1995, A1.

Foner, Eric. *Tom Paine and Revolutionary America.* New York: Oxford University Press, 1976.

Foner, Eric, ed. *The New American History.* Philadelphia: Temple University Press, 1990.

Franco, Barbara. "The Communication Conundrum: What Is the Message? Who Is Listening?" *Journal of American History* 81 (June 1994): 151–63.

———. "Doing History in Public: Balancing Historical Fact with Public Meaning." *Perspectives* (May/June 1995): 5–8.

———. "The History Museum Curator of the 21st Century." *History News* (Summer 1996): 6–10.

———. "Panel commentary." *In Museum Curatorship: Rhetoric vs. Reality,* ed. Bryant F. Tolles, 44–45. Newark: University of Delaware, 1987.

———. "Personal Connections to History: The Context for a Changing Historical Society." *Washington History* (Fall/Winter 1995–1996): 27–35.

Garfield, David. "Inspiring Change: Post-Heroic Management, an Interview with Harold Skramstad and Steve Hamp at the Henry Ford Museum." *Museum News* (January/February 1995): 32–34, 47, 49–51, 55–56.

Garfield, Donald. "Hard Money: Funders Talk about Funding for Museums." *Museum News* 74 (September/October 1995): 32–35, 51–52, 62–63.

Genovese, Eugene. *Roll, Jordan, Roll: The World the Slaves Made.* New York: Vintage Books, 1974.

Gibbons, Tom. "Americans' Knowledge of Constitution Slim." *Chicago Sun-Times,* 16 March 1987, 6.

Gilman, Benjamin Ives. *Museum Ideals of Purpose and Method.* Cambridge, MA: Riverside Press, 1918.

Glaab, Charles N., and A. Theodore Brown's *History of Urban America.* New York: McMillan, 1967.

Graham, Otis L. "Who Owns History?" *Public Historian* 17 (Spring 1995): 8–9.

Graymont, Barbara. *The Iroquois in the American Revolution.* Syracuse, NY: Syracuse University Press, 1972.

Grimes, William. "Tough Line on Grants for Arts: Shape Up," *New York Times,* August 5, 1996, 7.

Gurewitsch, Matthew. "The Brooklyn Museum Reaches Out—Again." *Wall Street Journal,* 15 April 2004, D6.

Guthrie, Kevin M. *The New-York Historical Society: Lessons from One Non-Profit's Long Struggle for Survival.* San Francisco: Jossey-Bass, 1996.

Gutman, Herbert. *The Black Family in Slavery and Freedom, 1750–1925.* New York: Pantheon Books, 1976.

Haskell, Thomas L., ed. *The Authority of Experts: Studies in History and Theory.* Bloomington: Indiana University Press, 1984.

Hegeman, Susan. "Shopping for Identities: *A Nation of Nations* and the Weak Ethnicity of Objects." *Public Culture* 3 (Spring 1991): 71–92.

Henretta, James A., et al. *America's History.* Chicago: Dorsey Press, 1987.

Herrmann, Andrew. "Attendance Down Last Year at More Than Half of the City's Biggest Museums," *Chicago Sun-Times,* January 29, 2004, 3.

Horowitz, Helen Lefkowitz. *Culture and the City: Cultural Philanthropy in Chicago from the 1880s to 1917.* Lexington: University Press of Kentucky, 1976.

Hoving, Thomas P. F. "Branch Out!" *Museum News* (September 1968): 15.

Janes, Robert R. *Museums and the Paradox of Change: A Case Study in Urgent Adaptation.* Calgary: Glenbow Museum, 1995.

Janzen, Mary. "Collaborative Risk-Taking: Making 'We the People' at the Chicago Historical Society." *Journal of American Culture* 12 (Summer 1989): 67–77.

———. "The Grant Process as a Tool for Exhibition Development—'We the People,' an NEH Success Story." Paper presented at the American Association of Museums annual meeting, 1988.

Jones, Charisse. "Museum's Walls Tell A Story of Division." *New York Times,* February 1, 1996, B2(N).

Kahn, David. "City History Museums as Social Instruments." Paper presented at Venues of Inquiry into the American City: The Place of Museums, Libraries and Archives. Chicago Historical Society. October 29–30, 1990.

Kammen, Michael. *A Machine that Would Go of Itself: The Constitution in American Culture.* New York: Alfred A. Knopf, 1986.

———. *Mystic Chords of Memory: The Transformation of Tradition in American Culture.* New York: Vintage, 1991.

Kaplan, Sidney. *The Black Presence in the Era of the American Revolution, 1770–1800.* Greenwich, CT: New York Graphic Society, 1973.

Karp, Ivan, Christine Kraemer, and Steven D. Lavine, eds. *Museums and Communities: The Politics of Public Culture.* Washington, D.C.: Smithsonian Institution Press, 1992.

Karp, Ivan, and Steven D. Lavine, eds. *Exhibiting Cultures: The Poetics and Politics of Museum Display.* Washington, D.C.: Smithsonian Institution Press, 1991.

Kavanagh, Gaynor. *History Curatorship.* Washington, D.C.: Smithsonian Press, 1990.

Kent, Henry Watson, ed. *What I Am Pleased to Call My Education.* New York: Grolier Club, 1949.

Kessler-Harris, Alice. "Social History." In *The New American History,* ed. Eric Foner, 231–55. Philadelphia: Temple University Press, 1997.

Kimmelman, Michael. "Culture and Race: Still on America's Mind," *New York Times,* 9 November 1995, B2(N).

Klein, Larry. "Team Players." *Museum News* 70 (March/April 1991): 44–45.

Korn, Randi. "Self-Portrait: First Know Thyself, Then Serve Your Public." *Museum News* (January/February 2004): 33–35, 50–52.

Krucoff, Carole. "Renovating the Society's Fort Dearborn Exhibit." *Chicago History* 9 (Summer 1980): 118–19.

Kyvig, David. "The Constitution at 200: Historicism or Useful Public History?" *Public Historian* 10 (Winter 1988): 51–59.

Lapsansky, Emma. "City Museums as Sources." Paper presented at Venues of Inquiry into the American City: The Place of Museums, Libraries and Archives. Chicago Historical Society, October 29–30, 1990.

Lavine, Steven. "Museums and Multiculturalism: Who Has Control?" *Museum News* 68 (March/April 1989): 34–36.

Lemisch, Jesse. "The Radicalism of the Inarticulate: Merchant Seamen in the Politics of Revolutionary America." In *Dissent: Explorations in the History of American Radicalism,* ed. Alfred Young, 37–82. DeKalb: Northern Illinois University Press, 1968.

Leo Burnett Company, Inc. "Chicago Historical Society, Part I: Aware Non-Visitors, Visitors," June 1988.

———. "Chicago Historical Society, Part II: New Members, Continuing Members, Lapsed Members," June 1988.

Leon, Warren. "Some Thoughts on Museums and the Constitution." *Museum News* 66 (August 1987): 25–26.

Leon, Warren, and Roy Rosenzweig, eds. *History Museums in the United States: A Critical Assessment.* Urbana: University of Illinois Press, 1989.

Lerner, Gerda. *The Majority Finds Its Past.* New York: Oxford University Press, 1979.

Linenthal, Edward. *Sacred Ground: Americans and Their Battlefields.* Urbana: University of Illinois Press, 1991.

Little, Cynthia Jeffress. "Beyond Text Panels and Labels: Education and Public Programming in American Historical Societies." *Pennsylvania Magazine of History and Biography* 114 (January 1990): 83–95.

Loewen, James W. *Lies My Teacher Told Me: Everything Your American History Textbook Got Wrong.* New York: New Press, 1995.

Low, Theodore. *The Museum as a Social Instrument: A Study Undertaken for the Committee on Education of the American Association of Museums.* New York: Metropolitan Museum of Art, 1942.

Lumley, Robert, ed. *The Museum Time Machine.* New York: Routledge, 1988.

Maehara, Paulette V. "Giving in America: Six New Trends in Fundraising." *Museum News* (March/April 2003): 35–37, 62–65.

———. "Seeing the Forest: The New Donor Demographics." *Museum News* (September/October 2003): 32–35.

Mariner, Dorothy A. "Professionalizing the Museum Worker." *Museum News* 50 (June 1972): 14–20.

Mathers, Kathryn. *Museums, Galleries and New Audiences.* London: Art and Society, 1996.

Mayer, Harold M., and Richard C. Wade. *Chicago: Growth of a Metropolis.* Chicago: University of Chicago Press, 1969.

Mayo, Edith P. "Exhibiting Politics." *Museum News* (September/October 1992): 50–51.

McCormick, Brian. "Gallery of Competition." *Crain's Chicago Business,* 29 September 2003.

McDonald, Pamela Mays. "The Bay Area Research Project: A Review through the Dark Eyes of One Hundred Years Ago." Paper presented at Audience Development: Marketing for Diverse Audiences. Graduate Department of Museum Studies, John F. Kennedy University, n.d.

McDonald, Robert R. "9/11: The World Transformed." *Museum News* (November/December 2001): 34–37, 62–65.

McKelvey, Blake. "Legacy." *Urban History Newsletter* 1 (March 1989): 4.

Menand, Louis. "The Trashing of Professionalism." *New York Times Magazine,* March 5, 1995, 41–43.

Metro Chicago Information Center (MCIC). "The Chicago Historical Society," 1995.

———. "Chicago Tourism Profile: A Report on Tourist Surveys Undertaken at Cultural and Non-Cultural Destinations in the Chicago Area," 1995.

Miller, James William. "Museums and the Academy: Toward Building an Alliance." *Journal of American Culture* 12 (Summer 1989): 1–6.

Morgan, Edmund S. *The Birth of the Republic, 1763–1789.* Chicago: University of Chicago Press, 1956.

Mueller, Klaus. "Invisible Visitors: Museums and the Gay and Lesbian Community." *Museum News* (September/October 2001): 34–39, 67, 69.

Munley, Mary Ellen. "Evaluation Study Report: Visitors' Views of the 18th Century." Paper presented at the Department of Social and Cultural History. National Museum of American History, July 1983.

Museum Education Roundtable. *Patterns in Practice: Selections from the Journal of Museum Education.* Washington, D.C.: Museum Educational Roundtable, 1992.

Museum Management Institute. "Heroic Leadership and Post-Heroic Leadership." Museum Management Institute's Curriculum Materials, 1992.

"Museums: Firsts, Facts and Figures." *New York Times,* 19 April 2000. 20.

Nash, Gary B. *Red, White, and Black: The People of Early America.* Englewood Cliffs, NJ: Prentice Hall, 1991.

———. *The Urban Crucible: Social Change, Political Consciousness, and the Origins of the American Revolution.* Cambridge, MA: Harvard University Press, 1979.

Nash, Gary B., et al. *The American People: Creating a Nation and a Society.* New York: Collins College Publishing, 1986.

National Commission on Excellence in Education. *A Nation at Risk: The Imperative for Educational Reform.* Washington, D.C.: United States of Education, 1983.

National Endowment for the Humanities. "How the Endowment Works." *Eighteenth Annual Report (1983).*

———. "The Purpose of Challenge Grants." *Seventeenth Annual Report (1982).*

National Science Board Commission on Precollege Education in Math, Science, and Technology. *Educating Americans for the 21st Century: A Plan of Action for Improving Mathematics, Science, and Technology Education for All American Elementary and Secondary Students So That Their Achievement Is The Best In the World By 1995.* Washington, D.C.: National Science Board Commission on Precollege Education In Math, Science, and Technology, 1984.

Neal, Armita. *Exhibit Handbook for Small Museums.* Nashville: American Association of State and Local History, 1976.

Newkirk, Pamela. "Searching for the Black Audience." *ARTNews* (May 2001): 184–87.

Nichols, Susan K., ed. *Staff Development: Innovative Techniques.* Washington, D.C.: American Association of Museums, Technical Information Service, 1989.

Norton, Mary Beth, et al. *A People and a Nation: A History of the United States.* Boston: Houghton Mifflin, 1982.

O'Neil, Robert M. "The Constitution, the Supreme Court, and Youth." *Social Education* 37 (1973): 397–99.

"Other Exhibits in Chicago." *State Journal-Register* (Springfield, IL), 9 November 2003, 27.

Parel, Rob. "Chicago's Immigrants Break Old Patterns." Migration Information Source, at http://www.migrationinformation/org/USfocus/display.cfm?ID=160.

Phillips, Charles, and Patricia Hogan, eds. *The Wages of History: The AASLH Employment Trends and Salary Survey.* Nashville: American Association for State and Local History, 1984.

———. *Who Cares for America's Heritage?* Nashville: American Association for State and Local History, 1984.

Pogrebin, Robin. "New York Arts Being Cut Back in Money Pinch." *New York Times,* 11 February 2003, A1, B8.

Pridmore, Jay. "A Museum Comes of Age: Historical Society Tells City's Story." *Chicago Tribune* February 22, 1991, CN3.

Project '87. "The Bicentennial of the Constitution. A Look Ahead." *This Constitution* (September 1983).

Quarles, Benjamin. *The Negro in the American Revolution.* Chapel Hill: University of North Carolina Press, 1961.

Rabinowitz, Richard, and Sam Bass Warner Jr. "Directions for American Historical Societies" *Chicago History* 10 (Fall 1981): 180–91.

Reynolds, Barrie. "Are Curators Second-Class Citizens?" *Museum News* 52 (May 1974): 33–35.

Ripley, S. Dillon. *The Sacred Grove: Essays on Museums.* New York: Simon and Schuster, 1969.

Rothman, Hal K. "Museums and Academics: Thoughts toward an Ethic of Cooperation." *Journal of American Culture* 12 (Summer 1989): 35–41.

Ruffins, Fath Davis. "An Elegant Metaphor." *Museum News* 64 (October 1985): 54–59.

Schlereth, Thomas. "Causing Conflict, Doing Violence." *Museum News* (October 1984): 45–52.

Schlesinger, Arthur. "The City in American History." *Mississippi Valley Historical Review* (June 1940): 43–66.

Schoener, Allon, ed. *Harlem on My Mind: Cultural Capital of Black America, 1900–1968.* New York: Metropolitan Museum of Art, 1995.

Schroeder, Cherry. "Diverse Audiences: How Do We Get 'Em into the Museum?" *Museum Education* (Getty Museum newsletter), n.d.

Schuster, J. Mark David. *The Audience for American Art Museums.* Washington, D.C.: Seven Locks Press, 1992.

Shafroth, Frank. "Deep Cuts: The Crisis in State Funding." *Museum News* (July/August 2003): 30–33.

Silvestro, Clement. "The Candy Man's Mixed Bag." *Chicago History* 2 (Fall 1972): 86–99.

Sozanski, Edward J. "View of the West Raises Hackles in Congress." *Philadelphia Inquirer,* 16 June 1991, F1.

Starr, Kenneth. "A Perspective on Our Profession." *Museum News* 58 (May/June 1980): 21–23.

Storch, Charles. "Museums in an Ethnic Turf Battle." *Chicago Tribune,* September 14, 1994, N1.

"Suggested Qualifications for Museum Positions." *Museum News* 59 (October 1980): 27–31.

Tanner, Helen. *Atlas of Great Lakes Indian History.* Norman: Oklahoma University Press, 1987.

Terry, Paula. "New Roles Will Require Even Greater Access to Museums." *Museum News* (January/February 1990): 26–28.

Thernstrom, Stephan, and Richard Sennett, eds. *Nineteenth-Century Cities: Essays in the New Urban History.* New Haven: Yale University Press, 1969.

Tolles, Bryant F., ed. *Museum Curatorship: Rhetoric vs. Reality.* Newark: University of Delaware, 1987.

Tucker, Marcia. "Common Ground." *Museum News* 69 (July/August 1990): 44–46.

Turner, Terence. "Anthropology and Multiculturalism: What Is Anthropology that Multiculturalists Should Be Mindful of It?" *Cultural Anthropology* 8 (November 1993): 411–29.

Wallace, Mike. *Mickey Mouse History and Other Essays on American Memory.* Philadelphia: Temple University Press, 1996.

Waller, Bret. "Museum Training: Who Needs It?" *Museum News* 52 (May 1974): 26–28.

Washburn, Wilcomb. *The Indian in America.* New York: Harper and Row, 1975.

Whitehill, Walter Muir. *Independent Historical Societies: An Enquiry into Their Research and Publications Functions and Their Financial Future.* Boston: Boston Athenaeum, distributed by Harvard University Press, 1962.

Williams, Stephanie. "Giving a Voice to the Anonymous." *Chicago Reporter,* July 2001. http://www.findarticles.com/cf_dls/m0JAS/6_30/79250842/p1/articles.jhtml. Accessed February 17, 2004.

Wolfe, Michael, and Robert Ferguson. "New Money, New Demands: The Arrival of the Venture Philanthropist." *Museum News* (January/February 2001): 56–59.

Wright, Benjamin. *Consensus and Continuity, 1776–1787*. Boston: Boston University Press, 1958.

York, Byron. "The Pursuit of Culture: Founding the Chicago Historical Society, 1856." *Chicago History* (Fall 1981): 141–50, 175.

Young, Alfred. "A Modest Proposal: A Bill of Rights for American Museums." *Public Historian* 14 (Summer 1992): 67–75.

———. "'Ordinary People' in Great Events: An American Museum Experience, Chicago Historical Society." *History Workshop* 32 (Autumn 1991): 211–17.

Young, Alfred, ed. *The American Revolution: Explorations in the History of American Radicalism*. DeKalb: Northern Illinois University Press, 1976.

———. *Beyond the American Revolution: Explorations in the History of American Radicalism*. DeKalb: Northern Illinois University Press, 1983.

———. *Dissent: Explorations in the History of American Radicalism*. DeKalb: Northern Illinois University Press, 1968.

Young, Alfred, Terry Fife, and Mary Janzen. *We the People: Voices and Images of the New Nation*. Philadelphia: Temple University Press, 1993.

Zamora, Herlinda. "Identity and Community: A Look at Four Latino Museums." *Museum News* (May/June 2002): 37–41.

Index